LARRY L. PETERSON BRUCE S. DAVIE

Network Security

A Systems Approach

SYSTEMS APPROACH LLC

PUBLISHED BY SYSTEMS APPROACH LLC

ISBN: 979-8-9937645-0-4

The cover photo of the Golden Gate Bridge is by Ziggy Stone and published on Unsplash at `https://unsplash.com/@pacnw`.

First printing, November 2025

Contents

Foreword

The Internet gave the world's population unprecedented access to information. Regrettably, it also connected the world's miscreants to the world's end systems. Not long thereafter, remote services relied on by users for critical tasks like banking, healthcare, and government concentrated vast troves of personal information on Internet-connected servers. The multi-decade steady drip of attacker-driven data compromises and service outages attests that these essential services and their data are attractive targets—and have been vulnerable ones.

Pervasive, fast connectivity and diverse, sophisticated services are some of the Internet's greatest successes. Internet security, by contrast, remains a uniquely enduring challenge. It was not a priority in early designs of network protocols and networked applications. It is also inherently adversarial: as one improves a system's robustness to attack, attackers adapt their "workload" specifically to target any remaining omissions or oversights. What's more, while users and service operators alike often value visibly new functionalities as "features" justifying increased complexity or cost, they may not as readily perceive security—roughly, the absence of undesired unauthorized operations—as a feature.

How should one approach building secure networks and networked applications that are robust and practical to deploy? A neophyte might expect that building secure networks is a matter of "just add cryptography." Surely, if one just chooses a good cryptography library and updates the implementations of existing network protocols to encrypt and sign messages, that's all that's needed.

Let's consider just a few of the many ways this simplistic view falls short of capturing the scope and complexity of secure networked system design:

- Cryptography requires keys typically associated with individual users, servers, and/or server operators. How does one distribute the right keys robustly and efficiently to billions of Internet users and servers that share no explicit prior pairwise trust relationship (e.g., where an online shopper has no prior relationship with the store's management or employees)?
- Suppose an adversary, while unable to view an encrypted message's cleartext content, records the encrypted message and sends an extra copy of it to the message's receiver. Any signature by the sender within the repeated message will still be valid. If the repeated message invokes an operation at the receiver (e.g., "Order an expensive item and charge the customer"), the consequences of the receiver's incorrectly acting on it may be dire. How can the original sender and receiver arrange for the receiver to detect and ignore such replayed messages?
- In the era of gigabit fiber to the home and 5G cellular connections, wide-area Internet latency often limits web and cloud app performance, rather than link speeds. Even a single added network round-trip in a communication can degrade user experience. As we secure communication protocols, how can we avoid adding network round-trips, so that server operators and users don't claim performance losses as a reason not to adopt secure designs?

It quickly becomes clear that designing systems that secure users' data and preserve service availability in networks like the Internet is a technically far broader and more subtle enterprise than "just add cryptography." In network security, not least because an adversary will actively seek out and leverage design lapses in any system component, a true systems approach is essential: one must reason precisely about the intended end-to-end security properties a networked application requires; consider how threats to those properties can plausibly manifest across the many components and layers of the full, end-to-end network system and in their interactions (on end hosts, at routers, and in the distributed Internet infrastructure, e.g., for route dissemination, name resolution, and TLS certificate distribution); and design robust defenses against those manifestations across all those components and layers.

This book fills a vital niche: it comprehensively initiates the reader into a systems approach to reasoning about network security, in all its depth and nuance. Peterson and Davie do so by introducing the fundamental design principles and toolkit of cryptographic building blocks that underlie secure systems, and then illustrating their application in a series of real-world, widely used secure network systems. At every step they lucidly explain from first principles why these designs take the form they do. Their treatment of recent developments of note in network security, such as 0-RTT session resumption in TLS 1.3 (a key technique for reducing handshake latency in performance-sensitive applications, already widely deployed), Passkeys and WebAuthn authentication in browsers (promising methods for moving user authentication beyond the pain of passwords, also already widely deployed), and ASPA for path validation in BGP routing (so recent that it is still an Internet-Draft) is particularly welcome. Their retrospectives on factors influencing uptake of secure designs for Internet name resolution (DNS) and routing (BGP) add rare insight into designing with an eye to incentive for adoption, beyond protocol technical correctness.

In an area as complex and subtle as network system security, it is unusual for a single volume to start with a discussion of elementary principles and progress all the way through to recent developments in the field, without compromising on essential detail or clarity. Peterson and Davie's meticulous explanations of a judiciously selected set of practically relevant secure network system designs achieve that, and are what make this book so rewarding.

Brad Karp
University College London (UCL)

Preface

The field of network security is roughly as old as networking itself. Conventional wisdom tells us that the original Internet was built without security features and we have been dealing with the effects of those design decisions ever since. It is not that the Internet's designers, implementers and architects were unaware of security concerns; many of them were directly involved in developing security technologies in early operating systems. But building a high-performance network that could scale to global proportions and accommodate the heterogeneous set of technologies that existed (and those still to come) presented more than enough challenges. To quote Internet pioneer Vint Cerf: *"getting this thing to work at all was non-trivial."*

Adding security capabilities to the Internet and the systems connected to it has been a multi-decade effort. While there have been some notable successes, such as widespread adoption of Transport Layer Security (TLS), vulnerabilities continue to be found and exploited. In part this is because security is a "negative goal": we are always trying to ensure that there are no more cracks in our defenses, and it is fundamentally impossible to prove that we are "done". So security continues to evolve as new weaknesses are exploited and new mechanisms deployed to prevent further exploits.

We have been educating ourselves about network security since we wrote the first edition of *Computer Networks: A Systems Approach* in 1995. There is an adage in security circles that no-one should write their own cryptography code because it is so hard to get right, and something similar might be said about trying to write a security book. It is easy to make mistakes, especially if you are not deeply immersed in the security world and the "look for every possible weakness" mentality. We've had to make a few corrections over the years to our security section in the big textbook. It is our perspective on security as viewed in the broader networking context that we have endeavored to bring to the topic.

So why did we decide to write the current book? First, we saw an opportunity to write about security in a way that would make sense to a networking person. Also, we wanted to take more of a systems approach to the topic. While we always try to take a system-level view in everything we write, it's easy with security to get bogged down in the details of individual components, such as cryptographic algorithms, without really tackling the systems issues. Cryptography is cool and interesting (in our view at least) but it isn't really the main thing to focus on if you are building secure systems. So while we do explain the basics of cryptography here, it's not the focus. We're aiming to explain how a system that comprises many moving parts, both in the network and the end-system, can be made secure.

This question of focus caused us to examine how much we wanted to say about end-system security. There are entire books to be written on operating system security, processor architecture bugs such as Spectre and Meltdown, and mitigating or preventing malware such as viruses on end-systems. We made a conscious decision to draw a line around the network and focus there, recognizing that, just as TCP is an important network protocol that runs in end-systems, protocols like HTTPS and TLS need to be covered in a book on network security. In fact TLS provides an excellent case study in the system-level issues that come into play when you try to secure traffic that flows between end-systems over the Internet, and we devote an entire chapter to it.

With the never-ending set of threats and vulnerabilities that need to be dealt with, it is all too easy to start thinking of security as just a collection of point solutions to the problems that have been identified so far. But in fact there is a well-established set of principles that have been identified and written down by pioneers in the field. The principle of least privilege and defense in depth are two noteworthy examples. We have dedicated a chapter to exploring some of the most widely accepted principles, and then we see them applied repeatedly throughout the book. Perimeter firewalls, for example, can be a part of a defense in depth strategy, while distributed firewalls have been proposed as a way to apply least privilege to datacenter networks.

Inevitably there are security technologies and types of attack that we have not covered in this book. What we have tried to do is to give the reader a sense of the principles at work and the building blocks that exist to build secure systems, and then illustrate how the blocks can be assembled to tackle particular problems ranging from securing Web traffic to securing the routing system that underpins the Internet. Security is a never-ending set of challenges and there will always be new threats and solutions. This book aims to lay the foundation so you can understand the network security landscape as it continues to evolve.

Acknowledgements

Thanks to all the people who provided feedback on our book at various stages in its development, particularly the following people:

- Brad Karp
- Cecilia Testart
- Zack Williams
- John Kristoff
- Motonori Shindo
- Nick Feamster

Chapter 1. Introduction

Security has been a focus of system designers for as long as we have had time-shared computers. If two users can share a computer, then it is necessary to have protections in place to limit the impact one user can have on another. For example, one user should not generally be able to read the data of another user just because they run code on the same system. At the same time, when one user *wants* to share data with another, the operating system needs to support that in a controlled way. Similarly, multi-user systems ensure that malicious or poorly written code from one user cannot interfere with the operation of another user's programs.

Computer networks are, like multi-user computers, shared resources, and similar requirements apply. One network user should not be able to interfere with another user's traffic, and in general, a user sending data across a network wants that data to be protected from unauthorized modification or eavesdropping. At the same time, networks are typically used so that specific resources can be shared among users.

As we will see, the security of computer systems and the security of computer networks are closely related topics. And just as a traditional networking book needs to pay attention not only to the operation of switches and routers but also to a whole stack of software that runs in end systems, so the topic of network security demands that we look at both the devices that make up the network and the end systems that connect to it.

The Internet was created to allow users in one location to access computing resources in another. Those systems had their own security measures in place. For example, if you wanted to use the Internet to log in to a remote computer, you would (usually) need to authenticate yourself to that remote system (e.g., with a user name and password) before gaining access to any resources on that system.

Ensuring the security of end systems, while important, does not come close to addressing the entire set of security issues that exist in a computer network. For example, an attacker with access to a link, switch or router somewhere in the network has the potential to read or modify packets passing through that point. Furthermore, failures of end system security are exposed when we connect them to networks. By connecting computers to a global network such as the Internet, the opportunity to exploit vulnerabilities in the code running on those end systems is opened up to a much greater (potentially global) set of actors.

Thus, we can think of network security as having two main thrusts. First, we need to address the security challenges of a shared, globally distributed network. Second, we need to address the challenges of connecting end systems running imperfect software to a global set of actors, some of whom are bound to be malicious.

For an interesting retrospective view on computer system security, and some commentary on how far we still have to go, we recommend the paper looking back on the history of security in Multics from Karger and Schell.

Further Reading:

P. Karger and R. Schell. Thirty Years Later: Lessons from the Multics Security Evaluation.. Annual Computer Security Applications Conference (ACSAC) 2002.

An early example of a security failure in the Internet serves to highlight the breadth of the challenges included in the term "network security". The Morris worm, the first large-scale attack on the Internet, was launched in 1988 when the Internet was largely limited to universities and research institutions. While it was made possible by the fact that the Internet of that era generally allowed packets from any source to any destination, it was also dependent on a number of vulnerabilities in the software running on the end systems connected to the Internet. Like many future attacks, the Morris worm exploited multiple vulnerabilities. In this case they included weak or default passwords, a buffer overflow bug in a widely-used software tool, and a security hole in the Sendmail program. There is a comprehensive analysis of the worm's operation in the report from Donn Seeley.

Further Reading:

D. Seeley. A Tour of the Worm.

What we present in this book is a systems perspective on the security of computer networks. Our focus is on how to create networks that meet certain security objectives, such as protection against eavesdropping and modification of data in transit. The systems approach requires us to look at the entire system: the network components and the end systems connected by the network, as well as both hardware and software.

1.1 A Short History of Internet Security

The Internet architecture was initially created with essentially no security features. This was not because the inventors, implementers and architects were unaware of security issues, but rather because there were other, more pressing goals. As Vint Cerf, the co-inventor of TCP/IP said: *"getting this thing to work at all was non-trivial."* David Clark, the architect of the Internet, has said *"it's not that we didn't think about security... we thought we could exclude [untrustworthy people]."*

The Internet's architecture is often characterized as an hourglass, with IP being the narrow waist that sits between a wide range of networks below and a wide range of upper layer protocols and applications above. The narrowness of the waist refers to its limited functionality: global addressing and a best-effort packet delivery model. Conspicuously missing from that waist is any sort of security capability. The best-effort packet delivery model included a "default open" setting: if you knew the destination address of a host, you could send it a packet.

The Morris Worm served as something of a wake-up call to the early developers of the Internet by highlighting just how vulnerable it was. By the early 1990s the first *firewalls* had appeared, allowing the default "accept any packet from anywhere" behavior of the Internet to be changed in a controlled way. These devices, which remain common today, filter packets based on information in the TCP and IP headers, and can be implemented in both hosts and routers. By 1994 they were common enough that applications such as FTP (the file transfer protocol) were adapted to work with them.

Also in the early 1990s, the Internet was growing quickly enough to make it clear that IP version 4 (IPv4), with 32-bit addresses, would eventually run out of address space. The effort to create a new version of IP, known as IPng (next generation) before being officially labeled as IPv6, had a much larger scope than a simple increase in the address space. Among those working on IPv6 requirements, some argued that this was perhaps the last opportunity to significantly change the IP layer, and thus the time to address perceived shortcomings of the Internet. High on the list of such shortcomings to be addressed was security.

The security features that were proposed for IPv6 included headers to support encryption, message integrity and authentication. However, it became clear that such features did not require a new version of IP, only a way to add optional information to the packet header, and so these capabilities also made their way into IPv4. These extensions became known collectively as *IPsec (IP security)* and are described in several dozen RFCs. We discuss them in a later chapter.

It is worth noting that, even if IPsec had existed in 1988, it would probably have had minimal impact on the spread of the Morris Worm. This is because the worm spread among hosts that were *supposed* to connect to each other (e.g., to exchange email using the Sendmail program). Encrypting and authenticating traffic between hosts doesn't prevent the spread of malware if the end-systems have the sorts of weaknesses exploited by the Morris worm.

The rise in popularity of the World Wide Web in the 1990s created the demand for security features at the transport layer to support applications such as e-commerce. This led to the creation of *SSL (secure sockets layer)* which was superseded by *TLS (transport layer security)*, both of which provided confidentiality and authentication at the transport layer. TLS is an important case study for network security, and we describe it in detail in a later chapter.

Another aspect of securing the Internet that started to receive attention in this period was the security of its infrastructure. One such piece of infrastructure is the *Domain Name System (DNS)*, which replaced static hostname-to-address mapping files in the 1980s, and subsequently become critical to the operation of the Internet. Clearly the information served up by DNS needs to be robust against manipulation by adversaries, and hence, there has been a multi-decade effort to add security to the DNS. The fact that this continues to roll on illustrates some of the challenges in making incremental updates to the distributed infrastructure of the Internet.

The Internet's routing system is at least as important as DNS, and similarly lacked any security provisions in its original design. Not only do we need to be concerned about modification of routing messages in transit, but it has historically been all too easy to simply send incorrect routing updates in BGP, the *Border Gateway Protocol*. For example, a router might advertise a good route to some prefix from an autonomous system that has no such route. Securing BGP has likewise proven to be a multi-decade, incremental task.

This is by no means a complete history of Internet security but it gives some sense of the scope of the problems faced. Some further perspective on this history, and the factors that contributed to Internet's lack of security, can be found in the following series of articles from the Washington Post, in which many of the Internet's pioneers are interviewed.

Further Reading:

C. Timberg. A Net of Insecurity. The Washington Post, May 30, 2015.

1.2 *Threats and Trust*

A discussion of security often begins with an analysis of the *threat landscape*. That is, what are the threats that our system is likely to be exposed to and which we hope to mitigate? This is one of the great challenges in developing a security strategy: how do we know when we have identified all the likely threats? Some may be obvious, such as eavesdropping on unencrypted traffic sent over a shared medium, but less obvious threats are constantly being identified. Furthermore, there are different *threat actors* with different motivations, ranging from those who enjoy the technical challenge of finding vulnerabilities, to criminals looking to obtain valuable information such as credit card details, to government actors looking to perform surveillance or interfere in elections.

It is common to talk about security as a "negative goal". That is, we are trying to ensure that a set of undesirable things cannot happen. That set of undesirable things is large, making security particularly challenging. Over the years, a number of principles have been developed to help manage this challenging landscape; we will consider many of them in subsequent chapters.

Noted security expert Bruce Schneier points out in his book "Beyond Fear" that security is also a matter of making trade-offs. You not only have to identify the threats that you wish to defend against, but also to decide what costs you are willing to incur in mounting that defense. For example, encrypting every packet sent by a computer in 1970 imposed such a high computational cost as to be barely practical or required special hardware; today it is routine that every packet sent between a web browser and server is encrypted. Thus, the trade-offs around encryption are different than they were when the Internet was originally designed. And just as we consider the costs that security techniques impose on our system, we must also consider the costs they impose on adversaries. Much of security consists of finding ways to make those costs highly asymmetric, so that they are much higher for the adversary than for those seeking to protect their systems and information.

Schneier describes a set of questions to be addressed in developing a security strategy:

- Step 1: What assets are you trying to protect?
- Step 2: What are the risks to these assets?
- Step 3: How well does the security solution mitigate those risks?
- Step 4: What other risks does the security solution cause?
- Step 5: What costs and trade-offs does the security solution impose?

Schneier's book is targeted at a general audience, addressing security in a broad context (e.g., airports), not just computing systems and networks. Nevertheless, it provides some useful guidelines that are applicable to system security.

Further Reading:

B. Schneier. Beyond Fear: Thinking Sensibly About Security in an Uncertain World. Copernicus Books, 2003.

It is also important to recognize that threats and trust are two sides of the same coin. A threat is a potential failure scenario that you design your system to avoid, and trust is an assumption you make about how external actors and internal components you build upon will behave. For example, if you plan to transmit messages over Wi-Fi on an open campus, you would likely identify an eavesdropper that can intercept messages as a threat (and adopt some of the methods discussed in this book as a countermeasure). But if you are planning to transmit messages over a fiber link between two servers in a locked machine room, you might trust that channel is secure, and so take no additional steps. Every system makes trust assumptions. The key is to be as explicit as possible about those assumptions, because they may change over time.

Taking this thought process a step further, trust assumptions aren't always as clear-cut as our strawman suggests. For example, most of us implicitly trust that the computer we just bought from a reputable vendor does not forward our data to an adversary, but for some use cases, the hardware supply chain is a consideration. Buying time on virtual machines in a cloud only complicates this decision. Even when you trust the hardware, you might or might not trust the firmware or the OS (or you might trust it only when certain security enhancements are enabled). This illustrates a common design question that every system must face: what do you accept to be the *Trusted Computing Base (TCB)*? That is, what hardware and software components do you trust?

We revisit this topic in the next chapter, but given that this book focuses on network security, a reasonable starting point is to trust the hardware/software on the systems you control, and to assume all other systems you interact with are untrustworthy. But this definition is problematic in a service-based environment like today's Internet, where we often end up putting some trust in the network providers we connect to, and the cloud services we depend upon. In many respects, identifying a TCB that meets our needs is an important part of what makes security so challenging.

1.3 Threats to Network Security

Computer networks are, as we noted above, invariably a shared resource. They are used by many applications representing different interests. The Internet is particularly widely shared, being used by competing businesses, mutually antagonistic governments, and opportunistic criminals. Most of the world's information is stored on systems connected to the Internet. Unless effective security measures are in place, a network conversation, a distributed application, or an end-system storing sensitive data may be compromised by an adversary. Critical systems ranging from healthcare delivery to the power grid are at risk of disruption from various forms of attack.

A simple and familiar example of threats and mitigations is the secure use of the web. Suppose you are a customer using a credit card to order an item from a website. An obvious threat is that an adversary could eavesdrop on your network communication, reading your messages to obtain your credit card information. How might that eavesdropping be accomplished? It is trivial on a broadcast network such as an Ethernet or Wi-Fi, where any node can be configured to receive all the message traffic on that network. More elaborate approaches include wiretapping or planting spy software on any of the chain of nodes involved. The insertion of monitoring software might be performed by an operator with physical or remote access to a router (e.g., an employee of an Internet service provider). A vulnerability in the router's software might be exploited by an attacker to gain remote access. And in recent years there have been examples of "supply chain attacks" in which malicious software is inserted in some code, either open source or proprietary, that is subsequently used in another vendor's products. In other words, there are a *lot* of ways that the data in flight from your browser to the website might end up in the hands of an attacker.

While various steps can be taken to secure the devices along the path traveled by your data, it is relatively straightforward today to encrypt all messages such that even if an adversary has access to the data, they are unable to *understand* the message contents. A protocol that does so is said to provide *confidentiality*. Taking the concept a step farther, concealing the quantity and destination of communication is called *traffic confidentiality*—because merely knowing where traffic is going, and how much, can be useful to an adversary in some situations.

Confidentiality alone is not sufficient. An adversary who can't read the contents of your encrypted message might nevertheless be able to modify it. By changing a few bits, it might be possible to order a completely different item or perhaps 1000 units of the item. There are techniques to detect, if not prevent, such tampering. A protocol that detects such message tampering is said to provide *integrity*. Similarly, an attacker might capture a message and send it again at another time, which might cause a duplicate purchase, for example. This is called a *replay attack* and prevention of such attacks is a common requirement of security protocols.

Another threat to the customer is unknowingly being directed to a false website. This can result from a Domain Name System (DNS) attack, in which false information is entered in a DNS server or the name service cache of the customer's computer. This leads to translating a correct URL into an incorrect IP address—the address of a false website. It is also common to create websites with domain names that look like they might be legitimate. A protocol that ensures that you really are talking to whom you think you are is said to provide *authentication*. Authentication is separate from but also requires integrity, since it is meaningless to say that a message came from a certain participant if it is no longer the same message.

The owner of the website can be attacked as well. Some websites have been defaced; the files that make up the website content have been remotely accessed and modified without authorization. That is an issue of *access control*, enforcing the rules regarding who is allowed to do what. Websites are also subject to *Denial-of-Service (DoS)* attacks, during which would-be customers are unable to access the website because it is being overwhelmed by bogus requests. Ensuring a degree of access is called *availability*.

In addition to these issues, the Internet has notably been used as a means for deploying malicious code, generally called *malware*, that exploits vulnerabilities in end systems. *Worms*, of which the Morris worm is a famous example, are pieces of self-replicating code that spread over networks. *Viruses* differ slightly from worms, in that they are spread by the transmission of infected files. Once infected, machines can then be arranged into *botnets*, in which a set of compromised machines are harnessed together to inflict further harm, such as launching DoS attacks.

We will look further into these various classes of threats and the measures developed to mitigate them in the following chapters. For a solid introduction to system security we recommend the chapter below from Saltzer and Kaashoek. Their perspective is grounded in *Operating System (OS)* design, which is the context for much of the foundational work in security. In that setting, finding the right balance between sharing (so users can access each other's files) and security (so you can keep users from accessing your private data) is a central challenge. Security is easiest when the answer is always "no".

Further Reading:

J. Saltzer and F. Kaashoek. Principles of Computer System Design: An Introduction. Chapter 11. Morgan Kaufmann Publishers, 2009.

Chapter 2. Design Principles

In the preceding chapter we looked at some reasons why network security is a never-ending challenge. As security is a negative goal, we can never be sure that we have foreseen and prevented every possible threat. Nevertheless, there are a number of general principles that have been developed over the decades that we can apply to improve the overall security of our networks and systems. We discuss these in this chapter and see them in action in subsequent chapters.

In order to take a systematic approach to security it helps to have a clear view of our requirements. Once we have defined those we can consider the principles that can be applied to help us meet them.

2.1 Security Requirements

The first major requirement that comes to mind when thinking about sending data across a shared network is likely to be *confidentiality*. As noted in Chapter 1, there are many ways that an adversary might gain access to data in transit through a network. Confidentiality is the ability to prevent data from being read by anyone other than its intended recipient. This, for example, is what is required to prevent your credit card details being exposed when you enter then on a website.

Closely related to the confidentiality of data is *traffic confidentiality*. This is the idea that we don't want an adversary to be able to determine where or to whom we are sending traffic, or in what quantity. This presents some distinct challenges from data confidentiality; there is no need for network devices to see our data, but they generally must look at packet headers, which contain destination information, to determine where to send traffic.

The second major requirement is *integrity*, which is about having confidence that the information we're receiving is trustworthy, and for example, has not been modified by some adversary while in transit. Assuring integrity is multi-faceted, involving more than just "in transit" adversaries.

For example, we need to be able to verify that an item of data was sent by the entity that claimed to have sent it. This means we need to *authenticate* the sender. In the example of e-commerce, this is what allows us to know we are connected to, say, the website of the vendor we wish to patronize and not handing over our credit card to some impostor.

Authentication implies that we must have a concept of *identity*. That is, we need a system by which communicating entities, often called *principals*, can securely identify each other. This problem is harder to solve than it might first appear. How can we know that a website with a particular URL actually represents the business with whom we wish to communicate? Or how does a banking system know that the person behind a particular HTTP request is actually the account holder?

Integrity also requires messages be *fresh* and *timely*, which is threatened by the possibility data is captured and then retransmitted at some later time. This is known as a *replay attack*, where for example, we want to protect against an attacker repeatedly adding an item to a shopping cart. Thus, it is a common requirement to have some form of *replay prevention*.

The final major requirement is *availability*, which is simply the ability to access all the data we have the right to access. System failures, either benign or caused by malicious actors, restrict availability. Another common threat to availability is *denial-of-service* (DoS) attacks. The Morris Worm was an early example of an unintentional DoS attack: as the worm spread to more and more computers, and reinfected computers on which it was already present, the resources consumed by the worm rendered those computers unable. Networks provide a means by which data can be amplified by replication, allowing large volumes of traffic to be sent to the target of a DoS attack; thus it has become necessary to develop means to mitigate such attacks.

Picking Your Battles

In Chapter 1 we talked about trust and threats being two sides of the same coin, but another way to frame the discussion is that every secure system design starts with two lists: (1) those elements you trust, and so can build upon; and (2) those elements you do not trust, and so must treat as a source of threats that you defend against. But this is no different than for any system you build: you first identify the building blocks you plan to take as a given, and then you design a solution that fills the "gap" between those building blocks and the requirements you are trying to meet.

One way in which security is unique is that over time you may discover that you need to move items from the first list to the second list, as new threats emerge. To reduce this possibility, it is best to keep the first list as small as possible. On the other hand, if you choose to trust nothing, you may end up "boiling the ocean" (i.e., having to solve so many problems that you are unable to make any progress). Every system must pick its battles.

Because of our focus on network security, this book effectively starts with a list of trusted elements that includes commodity servers and L2/L3 switches, and ignores (i.e., declares out-of-scope) all the vulnerabilities those elements face and the countermeasures that go into securing them. Of course, as soon as those elements are located outside our control, e.g., in some remote service provider's network, we have to assume that they are untrustworthy devices capable of snooping on, modifying or diverting traffic.

As a consequence of these three main requirements—confidentiality, integrity, and availability—additional requirements are placed on the underlying systems we build upon, which brings us back to the idea of a Trusted Computing Base (TCB) introduced in Chapter 1. We generally have three inter-related requirements for these platforms, beyond their not being malicious (which is implied by our including them in our TCB). The first we have already seen: they must provide a local (component-specific) notion of *identity*, giving us a way to support multiple principals (users). The second is they must provide *iso-*

lation, protecting information belonging to one user from other users on the system. The third is they must enforce *access control*, limiting which users have access to what data, along with what operations they are allowed to perform on it. Providing these mechanisms gives us the foundation we need to then meet the confidentiality, integrity, and availability requirements as we communicate over the Internet.

2.2 *Broader System Requirements*

Understanding the requirements of a secure system is important, but security is just one of many requirements placed on any system. It's also important for systems to be reliable, available, scalable, performant, usable, manageable, evolvable, observable, and so on.

These system requirements are sometimes indistinguishable from security. For example, a retail system brought down by a security breach is just as unavailable as one brought down by a hardware failure or a software bug. Similarly, a video delivery system designed to scale up to handle a flash crowd may also able to scale to fend off a DoS attack. In practice, it can be difficult to pinpoint the root cause of a failure (was it malicious or benign) and the root source of workload (was it malicious or legitimate). The main difference is that it is generally possible to provision for legitimate workload and benign failures, which can be measured and predicted (although not always accurately), whereas malicious attacks are often less predictable (although they should be expected).

Where the broader set of requirements become interesting is when they are in conflict with each other, and tradeoffs become necessary. For example, making a system secure can add latency to every transaction. Similarly, keeping a system secure puts additional burden on users (making it less usable), with the flip side being that those users are often the weakest link in the security strategy. These tradeoffs do not need to force an either-or scenario—clearly, designing for both security and usability is desirable—but no requirement is absolute, or we'd simply secure a system by denying access to all users.

For our purposes, the main takeaway is that security is unique in that it is not just a requirement *for* a system, but it is often best viewed as a system in and of itself, one that must be usable, scalable, manageable, evolvable, observable, available, reliable, and so on.

2.3 *Principles for Secure Systems*

Given how long people have been trying to build secure computing systems, including networked systems, there has been plenty of time to develop some principles that improve the chances that the system remains secure. We outline some of the most well-known principles here and the following chapters contain examples of how those principles are applied in practice.

2.3.1 *Defense in Depth*

As we have noted, one of the central challenges in security is that we never know if we have done enough. Much as we try to defend against all possible attacks, there is no way to be sure that we've thought of everything. This is what we mean by saying that security is a negative goal: we aim to be sure that a set of things cannot happen, but we can never quite be sure that all vulnerabilities have been found and mitigated. This leads to the idea of *defense in depth*: layer upon layer of defense, so that even if one layer is penetrated, there are multiple layers of defense still in place. Only by getting through *all* the layers of defense will an attacker be able to achieve their goal (of stealing our data, for example). The hope is that with enough layers of defense, the odds of an attacker penetrating all of them becomes vanishingly small.

As a simple example, a corporation might make use of a VPN (virtual private network) to ensure that only authorized users can access corporate servers, and that when they do so over the Internet, their traffic is encrypted. However, this single layer of defense is prone to several forms of attack, such as the presence of malware on the remote user's computer, or compromise of the remote user's credentials. Thus, additional layers of defense are needed, such as internal firewalls between different corporate systems; tools to detect, remediate, and prevent malware on the remote users' systems; and multi-factor authentication to protect against compromised user credentials. This is just a short list of defensive measures that are commonly used, and would not on their own be considered sufficient. But the point to note here is the use of many overlapping layers of defense, with the aim being that, collectively, they raise the bar high enough to thwart the majority of attacks.

The fact that we read about breaches in which attackers succeed in gaining access to corporate systems and data on a regular basis might suggest that the battle is being lost. Certainly the challenges in defeating determined attackers are substantial. However, it is surprising how frequently it turns out that a well-publicized attack has succeeded because some relatively common defensive measure, such as multi-factor authentication, was not put in place correctly.

2.3.2 *Principle of Least Privilege*

The principle of least privilege has a long history in computer science, having been proposed by Saltzer and Schroeder in 1975 (see the Further Reading). The principle states:

> *Every program and every user of the system should operate using the least set of privileges necessary to complete the job.*

A common example of this principle in practice is to avoid running anything as root on Unix-like systems unless absolutely necessary.

In the context of networking, this principle implies that applications which access the network should only have access to the set of resources needed to do their jobs. The concept of zero trust, which has started to gain popularity as an approach to network security in recent years, follows closely the idea of least privilege. We return to this topic in a later chapter.

Interestingly, Saltzer and Schroeder explicitly mention "firewalls" in the section of their paper on least privilege, using the analogy from the physical world (a wall to prevent the spread of fire) before the concept of network firewalls had been invented. As we discuss later, it turns out that the widespread use of network firewalls for most of their history *failed* to follow the principle of least privilege, in that it is common to find large "zones" of a network where all machines have access to each other, even though this access is not actually required for the machines to do their jobs. Addressing this shortcoming required some innovations in the design of firewalls that arrived only in the last decade or so.

2.3.3 *Open Design*

Another principle codified by Saltzer and Schroeder is that of open design. It states that the mechanisms and algorithms that are used to implement security should be open, not secret. The idea is that rather than trying to keep something as large and complex as an encryption algorithm secret, it is better for that algorithm to be published and only the key(s) be secret. There are two reasons for this principle:

- It is hard to keep an algorithm secret, especially if it is in widespread use as is the case with encryption on the Internet;

- Making security mechanisms robust against all forms of attack is, as we have discussed, difficult. Thus it is better to have wide scrutiny of these mechanisms to expose weaknesses that may then be rectified.

The history of computer security is filled with cautionary tales related to this principle. In the cases where the principle is followed, subtle bugs in protocol design or implementation have been exposed and patches rolled out to mitigate them. Heartbleed, a bug in the widely used open source implementation of SSL, is a famous example. The consequences of the bug were serious, with as many as half a million Web servers being impacted, but it was a positive thing that the bug was found, reported, and remediated quickly.

If this principle is not followed, a design that is believed to be secret may in fact have been compromised (e.g. by reverse engineering), or may have flaws that have gone unreported but are nevertheless being exploited.

Another way to state this principle is "minimize secrets". For example, rather than trying to keep an entire algorithm secret, only keep secret the key that is used to decrypt with the algorithm. It is much easier to replace a key that has been compromised than to replace an entire algorithm.

2.3.4 *Fail-Safe Defaults*

The idea behind this principle is the default settings of a system are the ones most likely to be used, so by default, undesired access should be disabled. It then takes an explicit action to enable access. This is a principle that dates back at least to 1965 according to the Saltzer and Schroeder paper.

It turns out that the design of the Internet really doesn't follow this approach. The datagram delivery model of the Internet, by default, allows packets from anywhere to be sent anywhere. So to the extent that sending a packet to a system can be defined as accessing the system, the Internet's default behavior does not provide fail-safe defaults. Efforts to revert to a more secure default behavior include such old ideas as network firewalls and virtual private networks, along with more modern approaches such as microsegmentation and zero trust architectures. We will discuss these developments in a later chapter.

2.3.5 *Least Common Mechanism*

This principle states that the amount of mechanism that is common to more than one user should be minimized. The principle was originally articulated by Gerald Popek in 1974, where in the context of operating system design, he argued in favor of minimizing the number of mechanisms put in the OS kernel. A failure (or security breach) of such a shared mechanism would impact all users, and so it is better to provide it in some other way, such as a library running the user's address space. The failure of such a mechanism then negatively impacts only that user, and not all users.

The counter argument is that any mechanism that requires privileged access—e.g., accessing an I/O device or modifying a shared data structure—must be implemented in a common layer (i.e., the kernel), but even then, care should be taken to decompose the mechanism so as to minimize the sub-pieces that are common. Library OSes designed during the 1990s took this argument to its logical conclusion, reducing the "kernel" to its bare minimum, with most functionality one typically expects from an OS running as a library co-located with the application.[1]

In an OS setting, the principle of least common mechanism is related to the principle of least privilege since the common platform (kernel) runs with greater privilege. This is because minimizing the number of mechanisms that require elevated kernel privilege also minimizes the privilege required across all mechanisms that make up a system. In a network setting, the principle is related to the end-to-end-argument. That is, it is best to avoid putting functions such as encryption into the network when the user is likely to need end-to-end encryption anyway.

[1] While strictly adhering to the principle of least common mechanism, Library OSes are not widely adopted in practice, illustrating that security is only one of many system requirements taken into consideration.

Further Reading:

G. Popek. A Principle of Kernel Design. Security Kernel Panel at the AFIPS '74 National Computer Security Conference and Exposition. May 1974.

D. Engler, F. Kaashoek, and J. O'Toole Jr. Exokernel: an Operating System Architecture for Application-level Resource Management. SIGOPS Symposium on Operating System Principles. December 1995.

J. Saltzer, D. Reed, and D. Clark. End-to-End Arguments in System Design. ACM Transactions on Computer Systems. November 1984.

2.3.6 Design for Iteration

Given what we have said about the difficulty of knowing that a system is secure, a useful design principle is to accept that we will need to iterate, and design for it. A good example of this is in the choice of particular cryptographic algorithms for integrity protection or encryption. These algorithms are often found to be insufficiently strong after some number of years, perhaps due to a weakness in the underlying mathematics, or breakthroughs in algorithms, or just the steady improvement in computing power that happens over time. Thus, any protocol that is developed that depends on such an algorithm should be designed such that a change of algorithm is an expected behavior. We see this in protocols such as Transport Layer Security (TLS) which includes a set of procedures by which two participants negotiate the cryptographic algorithms to be used.

Recent developments in quantum computing have raised the issue that many existing forms of cryptographic algorithm may need to be replaced. While the timeframe in which such a change will be needed remains a subject of debate, the safe choice is to accept that cryptographic algorithms will periodically need to be replaced.

2.3.7 *Audit Trails*

Part of dealing with the impossibility of covering all possible security threats is to accept that sometimes we need to analyze what has gone wrong. This leads to the idea that security needs to be auditable (observable). For example, it will be easier to conduct a post-mortem of a breach involving compromised login credentials if every login attempt is logged, along with information such as whether the login came over a VPN, what IP address was used, and so on. Similarly it is very hard to prevent insider attacks, but suitable logging might both make it easier to detect such attacks quickly and to deter those who might undertake them.

In a different vein, consider the design of secure protocols. The specification for TLS (transport layer security) describes a large number of error conditions that may trigger alerts, and recommends the logging of all such alerts. Such logging would help in understanding if the protocol was subject to an attack that involved incorrect or unexpected messages. Given the complexity of negotiations that go on in security protocols (to establish cryptographic algorithms and parameters, for example) it is wise to assume that these may have subtle bugs, and a good set of audit tools will enable any such bugs to be detected and then remedied.

Of course, the audit mechanisms themselves must be designed to be secure. A determined attacker will, in all likelihood, try to erase their tracks, so logging for audit purposes cannot just be an afterthought; it has to be part of the design of a secure system.

2.4 *Best Practices*

Design principles help guide how a system is architected to be secure, but an architecture has to be implemented by an engineering team and run on a day-to-day basis by an operations team. Mistakes in the implementation or operational practices render the best intentions impotent. To this end, software companies typically establish a set of best practices for the entire software lifecycle, from design to coding, deployment, and operation.

These practices start by establishing the security metrics that the end result is to be judged by, along with the processes used to review designs and test compliance. On the development side, emphasis is placed on using cryptography standards and the best available protocols, platforms, and languages. It is **not** an engineer's job to reinvent the security mechanisms described in this book, but rather, to know what mechanisms are available and how to use them. Once a system is deployed and operational, the emphasis is on proactively monitoring the system for anomalous behavior and establishing an incident response plan to deal with suspected attacks. Continuously collecting data about a running system is commonplace, and using AI/ML to detect (and potentially respond to) attacks is becoming increasingly common.

The details of these procedures is beyond the scope of this book, except as we note, that they depend on engineers and operators being well-informed about available security mechanisms. For an example of industry practices, we recommend Microsoft's Security Development Lifecycle (SDL) practices.

Further Reading:

Microsoft Security Development Lifecycle (SDL) (`https://www.microsoft.com/en-us/securityengineering/sdl`).

2.5 *Summary*

Just as we can never be quite sure that we have covered all possible vectors of attack against a system, there is no hard limit to the set of principles that can be applied to developing secure systems. The principles covered above include several that were drawn from the influential paper by Saltzer and Schroeder from 1975. That is the same Saltzer whose book (with Kaashoek) we referred to in Chapter 1. The fact that many of the principles from the 1975 paper reappear in the 2009 book is probably a sign that Saltzer had some confidence that these principles have stood the test of time. We recommend reading the entire paper.

Further Reading:

J. Saltzer and M. Schroeder. The Protection of Information in Computer Systems. In Proceedings of the IEEE, 1975.

Chapter 3. Cryptographic Primitives

In the first two chapters we have seen that network security is a multi-faceted problem. One of the major threats that must be addressed is that data traversing a network is prone to being read or modified by an attacker. The foundational technology for tackling such threats is cryptography. So we begin our study of technical approaches to network security with an overview of cryptography.

We introduce the concepts of cryptography-based security step by step. The first step is the cryptographic algorithms—ciphers and cryptographic hashes—that are introduced in this chapter. Such algorithms are not a solution in themselves, but provide building blocks from which a solution can be built. For example, cryptographic algorithms are parameterized by *keys*, with the distribution of keys a challenge that we tackle in the next chapter.

Once we have a set of cryptographic algorithms and a way to distribute keys, we are in a position to build protocols that enable secure communication between participants. Later chapters describes several such security protocols, culminating in the description of complete systems that use these protocols.

3.1 Principles of Ciphers

Encryption transforms a message in such a way that it becomes unintelligible to any party that does not have the secret of how to reverse the transformation. The sender applies an *encryption* function to the original *plaintext* message, resulting in a *ciphertext* message that is sent over the network, as shown in Figure 1. The receiver applies a *decryption* function—the inverse of the encryption function—to recover the original plaintext. The ciphertext transmitted across the network is unintelligible to any eavesdropper, assuming the eavesdropper doesn't have the means to perform the decryption function. The transformation represented by an encryption function and its corresponding decryption function is called a *cipher*.

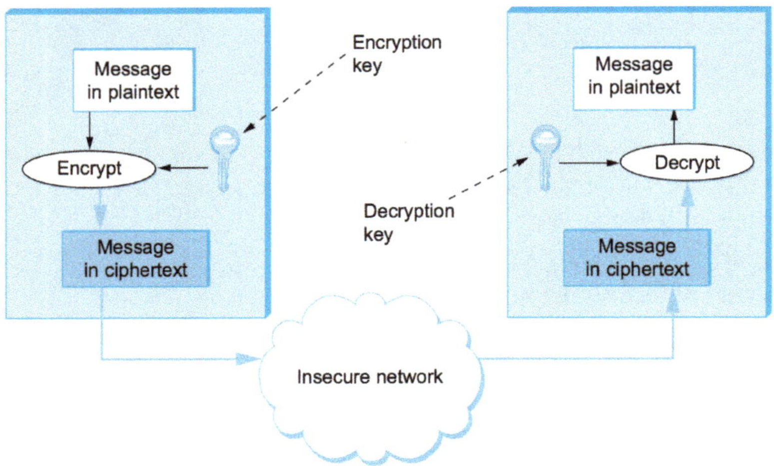

Figure 1: Secret-key encryption and decryption.

As we noted in the previous chapter, the principle of open design has been proposed for security technologies since at least 1975. Cryptography has a much longer history than that, however, going back thousands of years. One of the leading cryptographers of the 19th century, Auguste Kerckhoffs, stated in 1883 that cryptographic system designs themselves should not be secret, but should be parameterized by an easily changeable *key*; only the key should need to be secret. This also follows the principle from Chapter 2 of minimizing secrets.

One reason for open design is that, if you were to depend on the cipher being kept secret, then you would have to retire the cipher (not just the keys) when you believe it to be no longer secret. This means potentially frequent changes of cipher, which is problematic since it takes a lot of work to develop (and establish the security of) a new cipher. In the pre-computer era, ciphers were often implemented by specialized hardware such as the Enigma machine; these could not be easily replaced, but were re-keyed frequently. Today's algorithms, while implemented in software, are the result of lengthy processes of development, testing, analysis and standardization; all of this makes the algorithms expensive to replace.

Because cryptography algorithms are expensive to replace, but are occasionally found to be vulnerable after years of use, they are typically treated as pluggable modules in the end-to-end security solutions described in the following chapters. In many cases, the algorithm is a selectable parameter of those solutions, which means the overall system does not become obsolete just because one of its cryptography modules needs to be deprecated.

Also, one of the best ways to know that a cipher is secure is to use it for a long time—the longer it goes unbroken, the better the chance that is is secure. As with security in general, proving that a cryptographic algorithm cannot be broken is a bit of a negative goal, and thus hard to do with complete confidence. Sometimes we may be able to prove that breaking a cipher is as hard as solving some well-studied mathematical problem such as factoring large numbers. Even then there may be problems of implementation that will only get discovered by the scrutiny of those looking at and using the algorithm. And in many cases, we just have to rely on the fact that no-one has yet found a viable way to break the cipher. Fortunately, there are plenty of people who will try to break ciphers and who will let it be widely known when they have succeeded.

Parameterizing a cipher with keys provides us with what is in effect a very large family of ciphers; by switching keys, we are switching to another cipher in the family. It is common to limit the amount of data that a *cryptanalyst* (code-breaker) can access before the key changes. This provides the attacker with less ability to break the cipher, for reasons discussed below. It also limits the damage done if the code is broken.

The basic requirement for an encryption algorithm is that it turns plaintext into ciphertext in such a way that only the intended recipient—the holder of the decryption key—can recover the plaintext. What this means is that encrypted messages cannot be read by people who do not hold the key. When we say "cannot be read" we are going to make some assumptions about the computational capabilities and time available to the attacker; more on this in a moment.

It is important to realize that when a potential attacker receives a piece of ciphertext, he may have more information at his disposal than just the ciphertext itself. For example, he may know that the plaintext was written in English, which means that the letter *e* occurs more often in the plaintext that any other letter; the frequency of many other letters and common letter combinations can also be predicted. With simple ciphers, this information could greatly simplify the task of determining the key. Similarly, the attacker may know something about the likely contents of the message. For example, the word "login" is likely to occur at the start of a remote login session, and common headers appear at the start of HTTP messages. This may enable a *known plaintext* attack, which has a much higher chance of success than a *ciphertext only* attack. Even better is a *chosen plaintext* attack, which may be enabled by feeding some information to the sender that you know the sender is likely to transmit.

The best cryptographic algorithms, therefore, can prevent the attacker from deducing the key even when the individual knows both the plaintext and the ciphertext. In the ideal case, the attacker has no choice but to try all the possible keys—exhaustive, "brute-force" search. If keys have n bits, then there are 2^n possible values for a key (each of the n bits could be either a zero or a one). An attacker could be so lucky as to try the correct value immediately, or so unlucky as to try every incorrect value before finally trying the correct value of the key, having tried all 2^n possible values; the average number of guesses to discover the correct value is halfway between those extremes, $2^{n/2}$. This can be made computationally impractical by choosing a sufficiently large key space and by making the operation of checking a key reasonably costly. What makes this difficult is that computing speeds keep increasing, making formerly infeasible computations feasible. Furthermore, such brute force searches are easily parallelized, meaning that an attacker can use general purpose GPUs (GPGPUs) or other machines operating in parallel to speed up the attack.

It turns out that it is not trivial to create cryptographic ciphers that can be broken only by brute force. For example, the original DES (data encryption standard) algorithm had a key of only 56 bits; when it became clear that 56 bits was too small, triple DES was introduced, using three rounds of DES each with its own key. It might seem that this increased the key size to 168 bits (3×56) but because of the 3-round structure of triple DES, an attacker in possession of a piece of ciphertext and the matching plaintext only has to search a key space of 112 bits. This depends on something called a "meet-in-the-middle attack". The details are not important here but it illustrates why cryptographic algorithms need to be designed carefully and evaluated by experts if they are not to contain surprising weaknesses.

Network security tends to focus on the security of data as it moves through the network—that is, data that is vulnerable for only a short period of time. In general, however, we should also consider the possibility that data might be captured for later analysis, or that some data might be stored in archives for tens of years. This argues even more strongly for a generously large key size to prepare for future computational advances. However we do also need to consider that larger keys tend to make encryption and decryption slower.

3.1.1 Block Ciphers

Most ciphers in use today are *block ciphers*; they are defined to take as input a plaintext block of a certain fixed size, typically 128 bits. Using a block cipher to encrypt each block independently—known as *electronic codebook (ECB) mode* encryption—has the weakness that a given plaintext block value will always result in the same ciphertext block (as long as the key remains constant). Hence, recurring block values in the plaintext are recognizable as such in the ciphertext, making it much easier for a cryptanalyst to break the cipher.

To prevent this, block ciphers are always augmented to make the ciphertext for a block vary depending on context. Ways in which a block cipher may be augmented are called *modes of operation*. A common mode of operation is *cipher block chaining* (CBC), in which each plaintext block is XORed with the previous block's ciphertext before being encrypted. The result is that each block's ciphertext depends in part on the preceding blocks (i.e., on its context). Since the first plaintext block has no preceding block, it is XORed with a random number.

That random number, called an *initialization vector* (IV), is included with the series of ciphertext blocks so that the first ciphertext block can be decrypted. This mode is illustrated in Figure 2. Another mode of operation is *counter mode*, in which successive values of a counter (e.g., 1, 2, 3, ...) are incorporated into the encryption of successive blocks of plaintext.

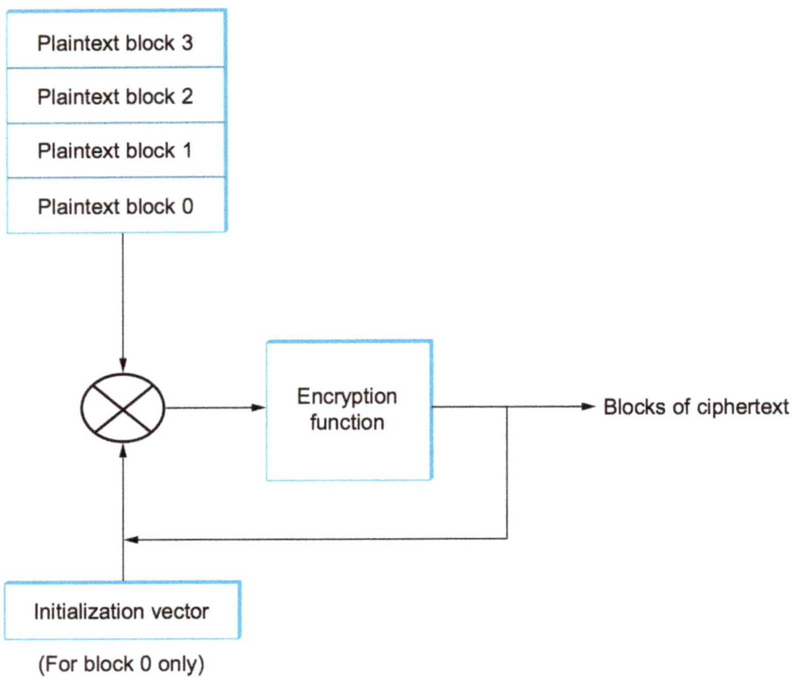

Figure 2: Cipher Block Chaining.

Block size, like key size, is a design tradeoff. 64-bit blocks were used for many years but as computer and network speeds increased and storage costs dropped, 64-bit blocks became vulnerable to a type of attack based on the *birthday problem* (the odds of 2 people in a group of size *n* having the same birthday being surprisingly high). If an attacker can manage to keep an encrypted session open long enough to receive two identical 64-bit blocks, they can gain useful information on the plaintext that produced the blocks. This was known to be an issue in theory for a long time but the exploitation of it was proven in 2016 leading to the deprecation of 64-bit blocks.

Block ciphers imply the padding of messages up to the next block boundary, which wastes some network bandwidth, so there is a cost to overly large blocks. For this reason most ciphers today have settled on 128-bit blocks. Some details on how the birthday attacks were shown to be an issue is available at the "Sweet32" website.

Further Reading:

Sweet32. Birthday attacks on 64-bit block ciphers in TLS and OpenVPN (`https://sweet32.info`).

3.2 *Secret-Key Ciphers*

In a secret-key cipher, both participants in a communication share the same key.[2] In other words, if a message is encrypted using a particular key, the same key is required for decrypting the message. If the cipher illustrated in Figure 1 were a secret-key cipher, then the encryption and decryption keys would be identical. Secret-key ciphers are also known as symmetric-key ciphers since the secret is shared with both participants. We'll take a look at the alternative, public-key ciphers, shortly. (Public-key ciphers are known as also asymmetric-key ciphers, since as we'll soon see, the two participants use different keys.)

[2] We use *participants* as a generic term for the endpoints of a communication channel. Depending on the layer of the network stack, a participant might correspond to a server, a process, a mailbox, or some other system abstraction. In the context of security, the communicating parties are often called *principals*, which in turn implies *identity*, and ultimately, an association with a human that can be held accountable. We use the term principal in place of participant when this full meaning is central to the discussion.

The U.S. National Institute of Standards and Technology (NIST) has issued standards for a series of secret-key ciphers. *Data Encryption Standard* (DES) was the first, and it survived for several decades before being deprecated.

DES keys have 56 independent bits (although they have 64 bits in total; the last bit of every byte is a parity bit). As noted above, you would, on average, have to search half of the space of 2^{56} possible keys to find the right one, giving $2^{55} = 3.6 \times 10^{16}$ keys. That may sound like a lot, but by the late 1990s, it was already possible to recover a DES key after a few hours. Consequently, NIST updated the DES standard in 1999 to indicate that DES should only be used for legacy systems. Importantly, DES was never shown to be vulnerable to any attack other than brute force.

DES was initially replaced by *Triple DES* (3DES). A 3DES key has 168 ($= 3 \times 56$) independent bits. As noted above, the computational cost of launching a brute-force attack was not, as expected, the cost of searching a 2^{168} key space, but rather a 2^{112} key space search due to the "meet in the middle" attack. At the same time, the computational cost to perform encryption and decryption was still three times higher than with single DES. This ultimately led to a process to replace DES with newer algorithms.

3DES is now deprecated in favor of the *Advanced Encryption Standard* (AES) issued by NIST. The cipher underlying AES (with a few minor modifications) was originally named Rijndael (pronounced roughly like "Rhine dahl") based on the names of its inventors, Daemen and Rijmen. AES supports key lengths of 128, 192, or 256 bits, and the block length is 128 bits. AES permits fast implementations in both software and hardware, being somewhat more efficient than triple DES. It doesn't require much memory, which makes it suitable for small mobile devices. AES has some mathematically strong security properties and, as of the time of writing, has not suffered from any significant practical attacks.

We won't go further into the details of secret-key ciphers, since it really is a field for specialist cryptographers. The security expert Bruce Schneier puts it this way:

> *Anyone, from the most clueless amateur to the best cryptographer, can create an algorithm that he himself can't break. It's not even hard. What is hard is creating an algorithm that no one else can break, even after years of analysis. And the only way to prove that is to subject the algorithm to years of analysis by the best cryptographers around.*

3.3 *Public-Key Ciphers*

An alternative to secret-key ciphers is public-key ciphers. Instead of a single key shared by two participants, a public-key cipher uses a pair of related keys, one for encryption and a different one for decryption. The pair of keys is "owned" by just one participant. The owner keeps one key of the pair secret. That key is the *private key*. The owner makes the second key public; that key is called the *public key*. Obviously, it must not be possible to deduce the private key from the public key.

Anyone can use the public key to encrypt a message they send to the owner of the keys. Only the owner has the private key necessary to decrypt the message. This scenario is depicted in Figure 3.

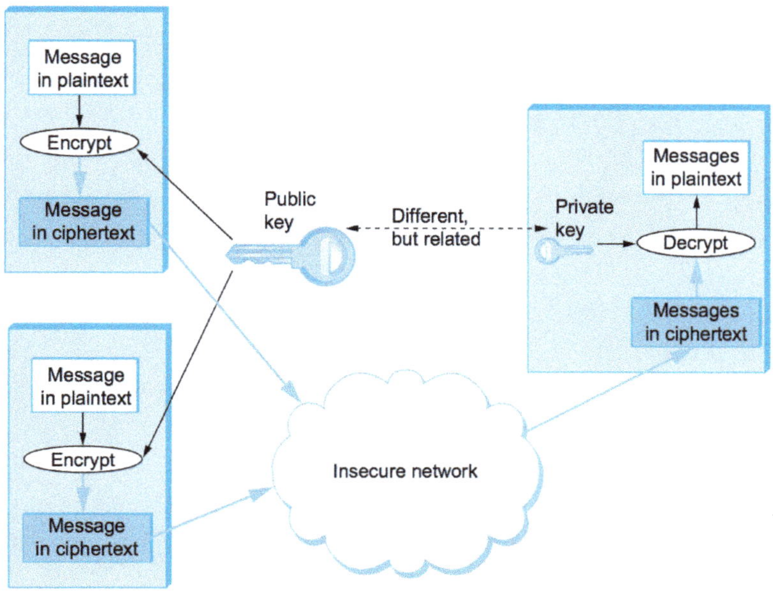

Figure 3: Public-key encryption.

Because it is somewhat unintuitive, we emphasize that the public encryption key is useless for decrypting a message—you couldn't even decrypt a message that you yourself had just encrypted unless you had the private decryption key. If we think of keys as defining a communication channel between participants, then an important difference between public-key and secret-key ciphers is the topology of the channels. A key for a secret-key cipher provides a channel that is two-way between two participants—each participant holds the same (symmetric) key that either one can use to encrypt or decrypt messages in either direction. A public/private key pair, in contrast, provides a channel that is one way and many-to-one: from everyone who has the public key to the unique owner of the private key, as illustrated in Figure 3.

Public-key ciphers are used not just for encryption, but also for authentication. The way this works is that the private key can be used with the *encryption* algorithm to encrypt messages so that they can then only be decrypted using the public key. This property clearly wouldn't be useful for confidentiality since anyone with the public key could decrypt such a message. This property is, however, useful for authentication since it tells the receiver of such a message that it could only have been created by the owner of the keys (subject to certain assumptions that we will get into later). This is illustrated in Figure 4.

It should be clear from the figure that anyone with the public key can decrypt the encrypted message, and, assuming that the result of the decryption matches the expected result, it can be concluded that the private key must have been used to perform the encryption. Exactly how this operation is used to provide authentication is the topic of a later chapter.

To summarize, public-key ciphers may be used both for authentication and to support confidential communications by encryption. In the latter case, they are mostly used to *bootstrap* confidential communications. Rather than encrypting the majority of messages sent between participants, public-key ciphers are used to confidentially distribute secret (symmetric) keys, leaving the rest of confidentiality to secret-key ciphers. The symmetric key sent over this confidential channel is called a *session key*. The reasons for this two-step approach include the higher efficiency of secret-key ciphers, and the need for reasonably frequent changing of encryption keys as described above.

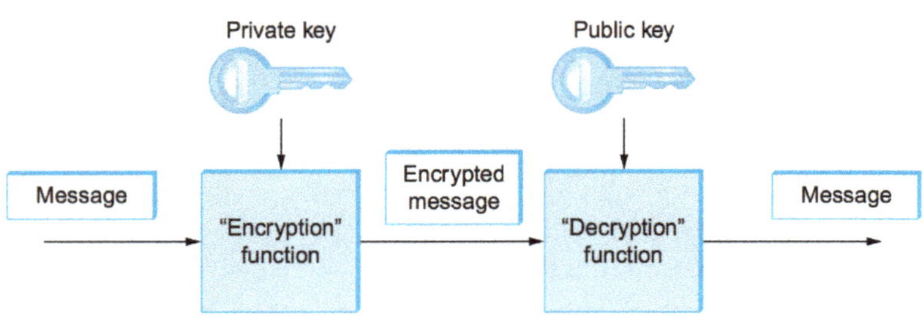

Figure 4: Authentication using public keys.

Public-key cryptography has an interesting history. The concept of public-key ciphers was first published in 1976 by Diffie and Hellman. Subsequently, however, documents have come to light proving that Britain's Communications-Electronics Security Group had discovered public-key ciphers by 1970, and the U.S. National Security Agency (NSA) claims to have discovered them in the mid-1960s.

The best-known public-key cipher is RSA, named after its inventors: Rivest, Shamir, and Adleman. RSA relies on the high computational cost of factoring large numbers. The problem of finding an efficient way to factor numbers is one that mathematicians have worked on unsuccessfully since long before RSA appeared in 1978, and RSA's subsequent resistance to cryptanalysis has further bolstered confidence in its security. Unfortunately, RSA needs relatively large keys, at least 1024 bits, to be secure. This is larger than keys for secret-key ciphers because it is faster to break an RSA private key by factoring the large number on which the pair of keys is based than by exhaustively searching the key space.

Another public-key cipher is ElGamal. Like RSA, it relies on a mathematical problem, the discrete logarithm problem, for which no efficient solution has been found, and requires keys of at least 1024 bits. There is a variation of the discrete logarithm problem, arising when the input is an elliptic curve, that is thought to be even more difficult to compute; cryptographic schemes based on this problem are referred to as *elliptic curve cryptography*.

Public-key ciphers are, unfortunately, several orders of magnitude slower than secret-key ciphers. Consequently, secret-key ciphers are used for the vast majority of encryption, while public-key ciphers are reserved for use in authentication and session key establishment.

Post-Quantum Cryptography

As we have seen, a lot of cryptography depends on the difficulty of solving certain mathematical problems, such as factoring prime numbers or computing discrete logarithms. When the efforts of mathematicians over decades to solve a problem have proven fruitless, it is tempting to declare these problems sufficiently hard for our purposes. However, there is a potential weakness lurking on the horizon, which is that many of these problems are known to have efficient solutions using quantum computers. Or more accurately, they could be efficiently solved on quantum computers that are much larger than any that have been built to date. As progress is made towards ever larger quantum computers, measured by the number of quan-

tum bits (qubits), there is a real risk that many current cryptographic algorithms will at some point become breakable.

There is plenty of debate about whether quantum computing will ever progress to the point that the risks to conventional cryptography materialize. Current quantum computers are much too small and lack the error-correcting capabilities necessary to solve the mathematical problems at sufficient scale, and it is not guaranteed that some version of Moore's law will apply to quantum computing. Building quantum computers that have a sufficient number of qubits and are sufficiently fault-tolerant to actually present a threat to cryptography remains an engineering challenge. That said, the risk is viewed as being sufficiently large that steps need to be taken to prepare for the day when quantum computers can break most existing algorithms. It is worth considering the possibility that some data that is well protected today could be stored for a decade or two and then decrypted by a future quantum computer, so even data produced today could be at risk.

The response to this uncertain threat has been to develop suites of cryptographic algorithms for which no quantum solution is known. This is the field of "Post-Quantum Cryptography". Note the use of the phrase "no solution is known". It is hard to prove that no algorithm exists—once again we are in the territory of trying to prove a negative. But NIST is running a process to evaluate and standardize a set of quantum-resistant algorithms, and there is plenty of focus on the candidate algorithms to establish their suitability over the long term.

There is a general, if not universal, sense that at some point post-quantum cryptographic algorithms will be needed. While the timeframe is uncertain and the exact algorithms to be used may change, the requirement for crypto-agility—the ability to swap out one set of algorithms for another—is now well established.

3.4 Message Authentication

Encryption alone does not provide data integrity. For example, just randomly modifying a ciphertext message could turn it into something that decrypts into valid-looking plaintext, in which case the tampering would be undetectable by the receiver. Nor does encryption alone provide authentication. In a sense, integrity and authentication are fundamentally inseparable. It is not much use to say that a message came from a certain participant if the contents of the message have been modified after that participant created it.

A *message authentication code* is a value, to be included in a transmitted message, that can be used to verify simultaneously the authenticity and the data integrity of a message. We will see later how such codes can be used in protocols. For now, we focus on the algorithms that can generate and verify authentication codes.

When data is stored or transmitted, it is routine to use error-detecting or error-correcting codes. These are pieces of information added to a stored or transmitted data object so the receiver detects when the data has been inadvertently modified by bit errors. Error-correcting codes are used on CDs and DVDs, for example, to deal with data corruption from scratches or dust. A similar concept applies to authentication codes, with the added challenge that the corruption of the message is likely to be deliberately performed by someone who wants the corruption to go undetected. To support authentication, the code includes some proof that whoever created it knows a secret that is known only to the alleged sender of the message; for example, the secret could be a key, and the proof could be some value encrypted using the key. There is a mutual dependency between the way the code is generated and how it is used as proof of secret knowledge. The following discusses several workable combinations.

For simplicity, let's assume initially that the original message need not be confidential—that a transmitted message will consist of the plaintext of the original message plus some additional code to support authentication. Later we will consider the case where confidentiality is also desired.

One common building block of message authentication is a *cryptographic hash function*. Cryptographic hash algorithms are treated as public knowledge, as with cipher algorithms. A cryptographic hash function is a function that outputs sufficient information about a message to expose any tampering. Just as a checksum or error-detecting code exposes bit errors introduced by noisy links or scratched disks, a cryptographic hash is designed to expose deliberate corruption of messages by an adversary. The value it outputs is called a *message digest* and, like an ordinary checksum, is appended to the message. All the message digests produced by a given hash have the same number of bits regardless of the length of the original message. Since the space of possible input messages is larger than the space of possible message digests, there will be many different input messages that produce the same message digest, like collisions in a hash table. An important property of cryptographic hash functions is that such collisions may not be produced deliberately under the control of the attacker. We will see why this is so in a moment.

A message authentication code can be created by encrypting the message digest with some key. That key could be the private key of an asymmetric cipher, known only to the sender, or it could be a secret key for a symmetric cipher that sender and receiver agreed to by some other means. On receiving the message, the receiver computes a digest of the plaintext part of the message and compares that to the decrypted message digest. If they are equal, then the receiver would conclude that the message is indeed from its alleged sender (since it would have to have been encrypted with the right key) and has not been tampered with.

Suppose that an adversary intercepts the message on its way to the receiver and tries to modify the transmitted message in some way. The message digest for this corrupted message would (with very high likelihood) differ from that of the original message. And the adversary lacks the necessary key to encrypt the digest of the corrupted message. An adversary could, however, obtain the plaintext original message and its encrypted digest by eavesdropping. The adversary could then (since the hash function is public knowledge) compute the digest of the original message and generate alternative messages looking for one with the same message digest. If she finds one, she could undetectably send the new message with the old authentication code. Therefore, security requires that the hash function have the *one-way* property: it must be computationally infeasible for an adversary to find any plaintext message that has the same digest as the original.

For a hash function to meet this requirement, its outputs must be fairly randomly distributed. For example, if digests are 128 bits long and truly randomly distributed, then you would need to try 2^{127} messages, on average, before finding a second message whose digest matches that of a given message. If the outputs are not randomly distributed—that is, if some outputs are much more likely than others—then for some messages you could find another message with the same digest much more easily than this, which would reduce the security of the algorithm. So a random distribution of hash outputs is an important property for these algorithms.

If you were instead just trying to find any *collision*—any two messages that produce the same digest—then you would need to compute the digests of only 2^{64} messages, on average. This surprising fact is the basis of the "birthday attack" mentioned above.

There have been several common cryptographic hash algorithms over the years, including Message Digest 5 (MD5) and the Secure Hash Algorithm (SHA) family. Weaknesses of MD5 and earlier versions of SHA have been known for some time, which led NIST to recommend a family of algorithms known as SHA-3 in 2015.

As noted above, the encryption of the message digest can be performed using either a secret-key cipher or a public-key cipher. If a public-key cipher is used, the digest is encrypted using the sender's private key, and the receiver—or anyone else—could decrypt the digest using the sender's public key. If a secret-key cipher is used, the sender and receiver have to agree on the secret key ahead of time using some other means.

A digest encrypted with a public-key algorithm using the private key of the sender is called a *digital signature* because it provides nonrepudiation similar to that of a written signature. The receiver of a message with a digital signature can prove to any third party that the sender really sent that message, because the third party can use the sender's public key to check for herself. Secret-key encryption of a digest does not have this property because only the two participants know the key; furthermore, since both participants know the key, the alleged receiver could have created the message herself. Any public-key cipher can be used for digital signatures. NIST has produced a series of *Digital Signature Standards* (DSS). The most recent standard at the time of writing allows for the use of three public-key ciphers, one based on RSA, another based on elliptic curves, and a third called the *Edwards-Curve Digital Signature Algorithm*.

A widely used alternative approach to encrypting a hash is to use a hash function that takes a secret value (a key known only to the sender and the receiver) as an input parameter in addition to the message text. Such a function outputs a message authentication code that is a function of both the secret key and the message contents. The sender appends the calculated message authentication code to the plaintext message. The receiver recomputes the authentication code using the plaintext and the secret value and compares that recomputed code to the code received in the message. The most common approaches to generating these codes are called HMACs or keyed-hash message authentication codes.

HMACs can use any hash function of the sort described above, but also include the key as part of the material to be hashed, so that a HMAC is a function of both the key and the input text. An approach to calculating HMACs has been standardized by NIST and takes the following form:

$$\text{HMAC} = \text{H}((\text{K}\oplus\text{opad}) \mid\mid \text{H}((\text{K}\oplus\text{ipad}) \mid\mid \text{text}))$$

where H is the hash function, K is the key, opad (output pad) and ipad (input pad) are well-known strings that are XORed ($\oplus$) with the key, and || represents concatenation.

A deep explanation of this HMAC function is beyond the scope of this book. However, this approach has been proved to be secure as long as the underlying hash function H has the appropriate collision-resistance properties outlined above. Note that the HMAC takes a hash function *H* that is not keyed, and turns it into a keyed hash by using the key (XORed with another string, *ipad*) as the first block to be fed into the hash function. The output of the keyed hash is then itself subjected to another keyed hash (again by XORing the key with a string and using that as the first block fed to the hash). The two passes of the keyed-hash function are important to the proof of security for this HMAC construction.

Up to this point, we have been assuming that the message wasn't confidential, so the original message could be transmitted as plaintext. To add confidentiality to a message with an authentication code, it suffices to encrypt the concatenation of the entire message including its authentication code. Remember that, in practice, confidentiality is implemented using secret-key ciphers because they are so much faster than public-key ciphers. Furthermore, it costs little to include the authenticator in the encryption, and it increases security.

In recent years, the idea of using a single algorithm to support both authentication and encryption has gained support for reasons of performance and simplicity of implementation. This is referred to as *authenticated encryption* or *authenticated encryption with associated data*. The latter term allows for some data fields (e.g., packet headers) to be transmitted as plaintext—these are the associated data—while the rest of the message is encrypted, and the whole thing, headers included, is authenticated. We won't go into details here, but there is now a set of integrated algorithms that produce both ciphertext and authentication codes using a combination of ciphers and hash functions.

If you want to get a deeper understanding of the principles of ciphers and hash functions, among other cryptographic concepts, we recommend the following book.

Further Reading:

A. Menezes, P. van Oorschot, and S. Vanstone. Handbook of Applied Cryptography. CRC Press, 1996.

Now that we have seen some of the building blocks for encryption and authentication, we have the foundations for building some complete security solutions. Before we get to those, however, we address the issue of how participants obtain keys in the first place.

Chapter 4. Key Distribution

We have seen that ciphers and authentication codes are parameterized by keys. So the communicating participants need to know what keys to use. In the case of a secret-key cipher, how does a pair of participants obtain the key they share? In the case of a public-key cipher, how does one participant know which public key belongs to another chosen participant? To answer these questions, we need to first understand that there are two different classes of keys to consider: short-lived *session keys* and longer-lived *predistributed keys*.

A session key is a key used to secure a single, relatively short episode of communication: a session. This might be, for example, a single HTTPS connection between a client and a server. Each distinct session between a pair of participants uses a new session key, which is always a secret key for speed. The participants determine what session key to use by means of a protocol—a session key establishment protocol. A session key establishment protocol needs its own security (so that, for example, an adversary cannot learn the new session key); that security is based on the longer-lived predistributed keys.

There are two primary motivations for this division of labor between session keys and predistributed keys:

- Limiting the amount of time a key is used results in less time for computationally intensive attacks, less ciphertext for cryptanalysis, and less information exposed should the key be broken.

- Public key ciphers are generally superior for initial authentication and session key establishment but too slow to use for encrypting bulk traffic for confidentiality.

This chapter explains how predistributed keys are distributed, and then explains how session keys are subsequently established. Note that session keys are a particular example of a shared secret, and in some cases there is a need for more than just a simple session key. In such cases we use the more general terminology of "shared secret establishment" rather than "session key distribution". The basic principles are the same.

We henceforth use "Alice" and "Bob" to designate participants, as is common in the cryptography literature. Bear in mind that although we tend to refer to participants in anthropomorphic terms, we are more frequently concerned with the communication between software or hardware entities such as clients and servers that often have no direct relationship with any particular person.

4.1 Predistribution of Public Keys

The algorithms to generate a matched pair of public and private keys are publicly known, and software that does it is widely available. So, if Alice wants to use a public-key cipher, she can generate her own pair of public and private keys, keep the private key hidden, and publicize the public key. But, how can she publicize her public key—assert that it belongs to her—in such a way that other participants can be sure it really belongs to her? It is not as simple as putting it on a public web page or dropping it in an email, because an adversary could forge an equally plausible claim that key x belongs to Alice when x really belongs to the adversary.

A complete scheme for certifying bindings between public keys and identities—what key belongs to whom—is called a *Public Key Infrastructure* (PKI). A PKI starts with the ability to verify identities and bind them to keys out of band. By "out of band," we mean something outside the network and the computers that comprise it, such as in the following. If Alice and Bob are individuals who know each other, then they could get together in the same room and Alice could give her public key to Bob directly, perhaps on a business card. If Bob is an organization, Alice the individual could present conventional identification, perhaps involving a photograph or fingerprints. If Alice and Bob are computers owned by the same company, then a system administrator could configure Bob with Alice's public key.

Establishing keys out of band doesn't sound like it would scale well, but it suffices to bootstrap a PKI. Bob's knowledge that Alice's key is x can be widely, scalably disseminated using a combination of digital signatures and a concept of trust. For example, suppose that you have received Bob's public key out of band and that you know enough about Bob to trust him on matters of keys and identities. Then Bob could send you a message asserting that Alice's key is x and—since you already know Bob's public key—you could authenticate the message as having come from Bob. (Remember that to digitally sign the statement Bob would append a cryptographic hash of it that has been encrypted using his private key.) Since you trust Bob to tell the truth, you would now know that Alice's key is x, even though you had never met her or exchanged a single message with her.

Using digital signatures, Bob wouldn't even have to send you a message; he could simply create and publish a digitally signed statement that Alice's key is x. Such a digitally signed statement of a public key binding is called a *public key certificate*, or simply a certificate. Bob could send Alice a copy of the certificate, or post it on a website. If and when someone needs to verify Alice's public key, they could do so by getting a copy of the certificate, perhaps directly from Alice—as long as they trust Bob and know his public key. You can see how starting from a very small number of keys (in this case, just Bob's) you could build up a large set of trusted keys over time. Bob in this case is playing the role often referred to as a *certificate authority* (CA), and much of today's Internet security depends on CAs. There are many commercial and non-profit CAs in widespread use today. You may also see CA expanded as *certification authority*—the two expansions are equivalent.

One thing to note about the above example is that we have to know two things about Bob. First, we need to know his public key so that we can verify that certain messages were originated by Bob. But we also have to know that Bob is trustworthy enough to make statements about the keys of others, which is where certificate authorities (rather than random individuals) come into play. We return to this topic below.

One of the major standards for certificates is known as X.509. This standard leaves a lot of details open, but specifies a basic structure. A certificate clearly must include:

- The identity of the entity being certified
- The public key of the entity being certified
- The identity of the signer
- The digital signature
- A digital signature algorithm identifier (which cryptographic hash and which cipher)

Certificates also invariably contain an expiration date. We will see how this feature is used below.

Since a certificate creates a binding between an identity and a public key, we should look more closely at what we mean by "identity." For example, a certificate that says, "This public key belongs to John Smith," may not be terribly useful if you can't tell which of the thousands of John Smiths is being identified. Thus, certificates must use a well-defined name space for the identities being certified; for example, certificates are often issued for email addresses and DNS domains.

There are different ways a PKI could formalize the notion of trust. We discuss the two main approaches.

4.1.1 Certificate Authorities

In the first model, trust is binary; you either trust someone completely or not at all. Together with certificates, this allows the building of *chains of trust*. If X certifies that a certain public key belongs to Y, and then Y goes on to certify that another public key belongs to Z, then there exists a chain of certificates from X to Z, even though X and Z may have never met. If you know X's key—and you trust X and Y—then you can believe the certificate that gives Z's key. In other words, all you need is a chain of certificates, all signed by entities you trust, as long as it leads back to an entity whose key you already know.

A *certificate authority* or *certification authority* (CA) is an entity claimed (by someone) to be trustworthy for verifying identities and issuing public key certificates. There are commercial CAs, governmental CAs, and non-profit CAs. To use a CA, you must know its own key. You can learn that CA's key, however, if you can obtain a chain of CA-signed certificates that starts with a CA whose key you already know. Then you can believe any certificate signed by that new CA.

A common way to build such chains is to arrange them in a tree-structured hierarchy, as shown in Figure 5. If everyone has the public key of the root CA, then any participant can provide a chain of certificates to another participant and know that it will be sufficient to build a chain of trust for that participant.

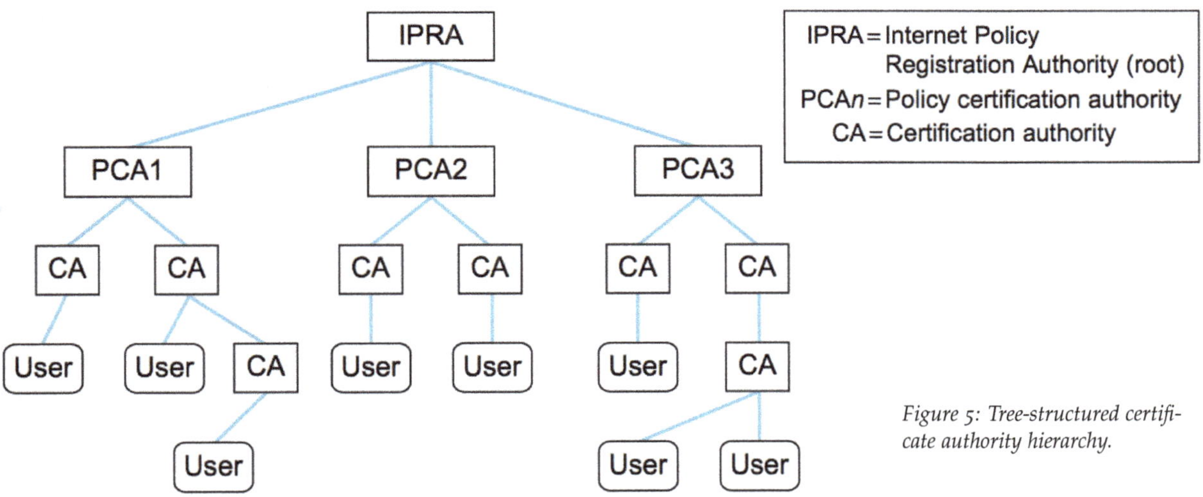

Figure 5: Tree-structured certificate authority hierarchy.

There are some significant issues with building chains of trust. Most importantly, even if you are certain that you have the public key of the root CA, you need to be sure that every CA from the root on down is doing its job properly. If just one CA in the chain is willing to issue certificates to entities without verifying their identities, then what looks like a valid chain of certificates becomes meaningless. For example, a root CA might issue a certificate to a second-tier CA and thoroughly verify that the name on the certificate matches the business name of the CA, but that second-tier CA might be willing to sell certificates to anyone who asks, without verifying their identity. This problem gets worse the longer the chain of trust. X.509 certificates provide the option of restricting the set of entities that the subject of a certificate is, in turn, trusted to certify.

There can be more than one root to a certification tree, and this is common in securing Web transactions today, for example. Web browsers such as Firefox and Chrome come pre-equipped with certificates for a (reasonably large) set of CAs; in effect, the browser's producer has decided these CAs and their associated public keys can be trusted. A user can also add CAs to those that their browser recognizes as trusted (or remove CAs from the default list). In other words, for most users, the browser manufacturer becomes the entity that they trust to look after PKI for them.

The certificates that are configured to be accepted by the browser are used by Secure Socket Layer (SSL)/Transport Layer Security (TLS), the protocol most often used to secure Web transactions, which we discuss in a later chapter. If you are curious, you can poke around in the preferences settings for your browser and find the "view certificates" option to see how many CAs your browser is configured to trust.

4.1.2 Web of Trust

An alternative model of trust is the *web of trust* exemplified by Pretty Good Privacy (PGP), which is further discussed in a later chapter. PGP uses email addresses (among other options) as the identities to which keys are bound and by which certificates are signed. In keeping with PGP's roots as protection against government intrusion, there are no CAs. Instead, every individual decides whom they trust and how much they trust them—in this model, trust is a matter of degree. In addition, a public key certificate can include a confidence level indicating how confident the signer is of the key binding claimed in the certificate, so a given user may have to have several certificates attesting to the same key binding before he is willing to trust it.

For example, suppose you have a certificate for Bob provided by Alice; you can assign a moderate level of trust to that certificate. However, if you have additional certificates for Bob that were provided by Carol and Dave, each of whom is also moderately trustworthy, that might considerably increase your level of confidence that the public key you have for Bob is valid. In short, PGP recognizes that the problem of establishing trust is quite a personal matter and gives users the raw material to make their own decisions, rather than assuming that they are all willing to trust in a single hierarchical structure of CAs. To quote Phil Zimmerman, the developer of PGP, *"PGP is for people who prefer to pack their own parachutes."*

PGP has become quite popular in the networking community, and PGP was eventually developed into an Internet standard known as OpenPGP. PGP key-signing parties were once a regular feature of IETF meetings. At a key-signing party, an individual can:

- Collect public keys from others whose identity he knows (often by collecting the fingerprint of the key—a short hash of the key—on a printed card.)
- Provide his public key (or its fingerprint) to others, perhaps showing some other form of ID.
- Get his public key signed by others, thus collecting certificates that will be persuasive to an increasingly large set of people.
- Sign the public key of other individuals, thus helping them build up their set of certificates that they can use to distribute their public keys.
- Collect certificates from other individuals whom he trusts enough to sign keys.

Thus, over time, users collect a set of certificates with varying degrees of trust and the web of trust can be extended and made stronger.

4.1.3 Certificate Revocation

One issue that arises with certificates is how to revoke, or undo, a certificate. Why is this important? Suppose that you suspect that someone has discovered your private key. There may be any number of certificates in the universe that assert that you are the owner of the public key corresponding to that private key. The person who discovered your private key thus has everything required to impersonate you: valid certificates and your private key. To solve this problem, it would be nice to be able to revoke the certificates that bind your old, compromised key to your identity, so that the impersonator will no longer be able to persuade other people that he is you.

The basic solution to the problem is simple enough. Each CA can issue a *certificate revocation list* (CRL), which is a digitally signed list of certificates that have been revoked. The CRL is periodically updated and made publicly available. Because it is digitally signed, it can just be posted on a website. Now, when Alice receives a certificate for Bob that she wants to verify, she will first consult the latest CRL issued by the CA. As long as the certificate has not been revoked, it is valid. Note that, if all certificates have unlimited life spans, the CRL would always be getting longer, since you could never take a certificate off the CRL for fear that some copy of the revoked certificate might be used. For this reason, it is common to attach an expiration date to a certificate when it is issued. Thus, we can limit the length of time that a revoked certificate needs to stay on a CRL. As soon as its original expiration date is passed, it can be removed from the CRL.

In practice, certificate revocation has proven to be challenging. CRLs can become very long now that certificates are in widespread use, so retrieving them becomes costly. The time to retrieve a CRL may fall in the critical path for opening a connection to a web site, substantially increasing the time to load a page. A determined attacker who has compromised a private key is motivated to disrupt the distribution of the CRL to prolong the amount of time they can use the compromised key. A number of proposals have been made to improve the effectiveness of certificate revocation, such as using bit vectors or other compact representations of the CRL to reduce its size, and the development of the Online Certificate Status Protocol (OCSP) to enable real-time checks on a certificate's status. At the time of writing, there are some best practices for handling certificate revocation but no comprehensive solution. A good discussion of the issues and a potential approach to more effective certificate revocation can be found in John Schanck's blog post.

Further Reading:

J. Schanck. CRLite: Fast, private, and comprehensive certificate revocation checking in Firefox. Mozilla blog, August 2025.

4.2 Distribution of Secret Keys

Secret key ciphers present a bootstrapping problem: how do you securely get the secret key to be shared by two participants? If Alice wants to use a secret-key cipher to communicate with Bob, she can't just pick a key and send it to him because, without already having a key, they can't encrypt this key to keep it confidential. Furthermore, if they can't authenticate each other, then Alice can't safely send the key to some unauthenticated recipient. As with public keys, then, some predistribution scheme is needed. Predistribution is harder for secret keys than for public keys for two obvious reasons:

- While only one public key per entity is sufficient for authentication and confidentiality, there must be a secret key for each pair of entities who wish to communicate. If there are N entities, that means N(N-1)/2 keys.
- Unlike public keys, secret keys must be kept secret.

In summary, there are a lot more keys to distribute, and you can't use certificates that everyone can read.

One common solution is to use public key operations to bootstrap the communication. This is how keys for symmetric ciphers get distributed in HTTPS, for example. We will see more detail of this later.

Another common solution is to use a *Key Distribution Center* (KDC). A KDC is a trusted entity that shares a secret key with each other entity. This brings the number of keys down to a more manageable N-1, few enough to establish out of band for some applications. When Alice wishes to communicate with Bob, that communication does not travel via the KDC. Rather, the KDC participates in a protocol that authenticates Alice and Bob—using the keys that the KDC already shares with each of them—and generates a new session key for them to use. Then Alice and Bob communicate directly using their session key. Kerberos is a widely used system based on this approach. We describe Kerberos (which also provides authentication) in the next chapter. The following section describes a powerful alternative.

4.3 Diffie-Hellman Key Exchange

A widely used approach to establishing a shared secret key is to use the Diffie-Hellman key exchange protocol, which works without using any predistributed keys. The messages exchanged between Alice and Bob can be read by anyone able to eavesdrop, and yet the eavesdropper won't know the secret key that Alice and Bob end up with.

Diffie-Hellman doesn't authenticate the participants. Since it is rarely useful to communicate securely without being sure whom you're communicating with, Diffie-Hellman is usually augmented in some way to provide authentication. Diffie-Hellman is used in both the Internet Key Exchange (IKE) protocol, a part of the IP Security (IPsec) architecture, and in Transport Layer Security (TLS).

The Diffie-Hellman protocol has two parameters, p and g, both of which are public and may be used by all the users in a particular system. Parameter p must be a prime number. The integers mod$p$ (short for modulo p) are 0 through p-1, since x mod p is the remainder after x is divided by p, and form what mathematicians call a *group* under multiplication. Parameter g (usually called a generator) must be a *primitive root* of p: For every number n from 1 through p-1 there must be some value k such that $n = g^k \bmod p$. For example, if p were the prime number 5 (a real system would use a much larger number), then we might choose 2 to be the generator g since:

$$1 = 2^0 \bmod p$$

$$2 = 2^1 \bmod p$$

$$3 = 2^3 \bmod p$$

$$4 = 2^2 \bmod p$$

Suppose Alice and Bob want to agree on a shared secret key. Alice and Bob, and everyone else, already know the values of p and g.

Alice generates a random private value a and Bob generates a random private value b. Both a and b are drawn from the set of integers $\{1, \ldots, p-1\}$. Alice and Bob derive their corresponding public values—the values they will send to each other unencrypted—as follows. Alice's public value is

$$g^a \bmod p$$

and Bob's public value is

$$g^b \bmod p.$$

They then exchange their public values. Finally, Alice computes

$$g^{ab} \bmod p = (g^b \bmod p)^a \bmod p$$

and Bob computes

$$g^{ba} \bmod p = (g^a \bmod p)^b \bmod p.$$

Alice and Bob now have $g^{ab} \bmod p$ (which is equal to $g^{ba} \bmod p$) as their shared secret key.

Any eavesdropper would know p, g, and the two public values $g^a \bmod p$ and $g^b \bmod p$. If only the eavesdropper could determine a or b, she could easily compute the resulting key. Determining a or b from that information is, however, computationally infeasible for suitably large p,a, and b; it is known as the *discrete logarithm problem.*

Let's look at an example using small numbers to illustrate the calculation. Let $p = 5$ and $g = 2$, and suppose Alice picks the random number $a = 3$ and Bob picks the random number $b = 4$. Then Alice sends Bob the public value

$$2^3 \bmod 5 = 3$$

and Bob sends Alice the public value

$$2^4 \bmod 5 = 1.$$

Alice is then able to compute

$$g^{ab} \bmod p = (2^b \bmod 5)^3 \bmod 5 = (1)^3 \bmod 5 = 1$$

by substituting Bob's public value for $(2^b \bmod 5)$. Similarly, Bob is able to compute

$$g^{ba} \bmod p = (g^a \bmod 5)^4 \bmod 5 = (3)^4 \bmod 5 = 1$$

by substituting Alice's public value for $(2^a \bmod 5)$. Both Alice and Bob now agree that the secret key is 1.

There is the problem of Diffie-Hellman's lack of authentication. One attack that can take advantage of this is the *man-in-the-middle attack*. Suppose Mallory is an adversary with the ability to intercept messages. Mallory already knows p and g since they are public, and she generates random private values c and d to use with Alice and Bob, respectively. When Alice and Bob send their public values to each other, Mallory intercepts them and sends her own public values, as in Figure 6. The result is that Alice and Bob each end up unknowingly sharing a key with Mallory instead of each other.

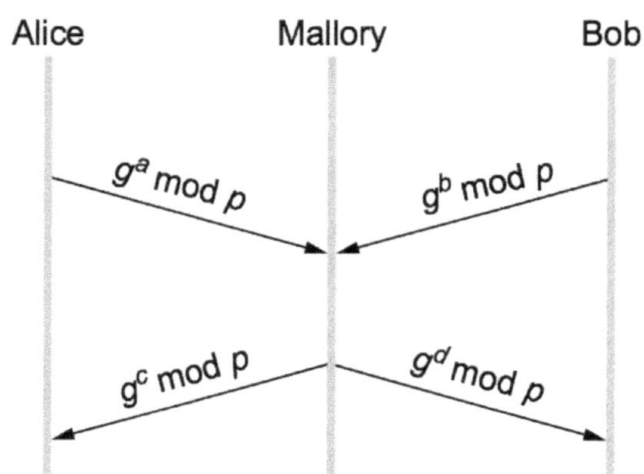

Figure 6: A man-in-the-middle attack.

A variant of Diffie-Hellman sometimes called *fixed Diffie-Hellman* supports authentication of one or both participants. It relies on certificates that are similar to public key certificates but instead certify the Diffie-Hellman public parameters of an entity. For example, such a certificate would state that Alice's Diffie-Hellman parameters are p, g, and $g^a \bmod p$ (note that the value of a would still be known only to Alice). Such a certificate would assure Bob that the other participant in Diffie-Hellman is Alice—or else the other participant won't be able to compute the secret key, because she won't know a. If both participants have certificates for their Diffie-Hellman parameters, they can authenticate each other. If just one has a certificate, then just that one can be authenticated. This is useful in some situations; for example, when one participant is a web server and the other is an arbitrary client, the client can authenticate the web server and establish a secret key for confidentiality before sending a credit card number to the web server.

A further variant of Diffie-Hellman, which is used in TLS, is called *ephemeral* Diffie-Hellman. Like the fixed variant, it relies on at least one participant having a certificate issued by a CA, but in this case it certifies that Alice is associated with a given public key (e.g., an RSA key). Alice then generates an ephemeral value of a rather than a fixed one, and uses her private key to sign the Diffie Hellman parameters: p, g, and $g^a \bmod p$. By providing the certificate and the signed value, Alice is able to show Bob that the message has really come from her and authenticate the Diffie-Hellman parameters, while still keeping a secret. Unlike fixed Diffie-Hellman, this approach provides *forward secrecy*, meaning that even if the long-lived private key of Alice were to be compromised, past sessions that had been recorded by an attacker will still be secure, since they used ephemeral keys that changed with every session. Note that while the word "ephemeral" strictly implies only that a is a short-lived value, it is widely used in protocol specifications to apply to cases where authentication is also performed using a public key as we have described it here. To avoid confusion, the original form of Diffie-Hellman that lacks authentication is often referred to as "anonymous" mode.

Chapter 5. Authentication Protocols

So far we described how to encrypt messages, build message authentication codes, and distribute keys. It might seem as if all we have to do to make a protocol secure is append an authentication code to every message and, if we want confidentiality, encrypt the message.

There are two main reasons why it's not that simple. First, there is the problem of a *replay attack*: an adversary retransmitting a copy of a message that was previously sent. One could imagine, for example, that a message in which you place an order for some item on a website could be replayed, appearing to the website as though you had ordered more of the same. Even though it wasn't the original incarnation of the message, its authentication code would still be valid; after all, the message was created by you, and it wasn't modified. Clearly, we need a solution that ensures *freshness*.

In a variation of this attack called a *suppress-replay attack*, an adversary might merely delay your message (by intercepting and later replaying it), so that it is received at a time when it is no longer appropriate. For example, an adversary could delay your order to buy stock from an auspicious time to a time when you would not have wanted to buy. Although this message would in a sense be fresh (it hasn't been sent before), it wouldn't be timely. So we also need to ensure *timeliness*. Freshness and timeliness may be considered aspects of integrity. Ensuring them will in most cases require a nontrivial, back-and-forth protocol.

The second problem we have not yet solved is how to establish a session key: a secret-key cipher key generated on the fly and used for just one session. This too involves a nontrivial protocol.

What these two issues have in common is authentication. If a message is not fresh and timely, then from a practical standpoint we want to consider it as not being authentic, i.e., not being from whom it claims to be. And, obviously, when you are arranging to share a new session key with someone, you want to know you are sharing it with the right person. Usually, authentication protocols establish a session key at the same time, so that at the end of the protocol Alice and Bob have authenticated each other and they have a new secret key to use. Without a new session key, the protocol would just authenticate Alice and Bob at one point in time; a session key allows them to efficiently authenticate subsequent messages. Generally, session key establishment protocols perform authentication. As we noted in the last chapter, Diffie-Hellman key exchange in its simplest form does not provide authentication, but in practical usage it is almost always combined with an authentication protocol.

There is a core set of techniques used to ensure freshness and timeliness in authentication protocols. We describe those techniques before moving on to particular protocols.

5.1 Freshness and Timeliness Techniques

We have seen that authentication codes alone do not enable us to detect messages that are not fresh or timely. One approach is to include a timestamp in the message. Obviously the timestamp itself must be tamperproof, so it must be covered by the message authentication code. The primary drawback to timestamps is that they require distributed clock synchronization. Since our system would then depend on synchronization, the clock synchronization itself would need to be defended against security threats, in addition to the usual challenges of clock synchronization. Another issue is that distributed clocks are synchronized to only a certain degree—a certain margin of error. Thus, the timing integrity provided by timestamps is only as good as the degree of synchronization.

Another approach is to include a *nonce*—a random number used only once—in the message. Participants can then detect replay attacks by checking whether a nonce has been used previously. On its own, this would require keeping track of past nonces, of which a great many could accumulate.

A solution to the shortcomings of timestamps and nonces is to use one or both of them in a *challenge-response* protocol. Suppose we use a timestamp. In a challenge-response protocol, Alice sends Bob a timestamp, challenging Bob to encrypt it in a response message (if they share a secret key) or digitally sign it in a response message (if Bob has a public key, as in Figure 7). The encrypted timestamp is like an authentication code that additionally proves timeliness. Alice can easily check the timeliness of the timestamp in a response from Bob since that timestamp comes from Alice's own clock—no distributed clock synchronization needed. Suppose instead that the protocol uses nonces. Then Alice need only keep track of those nonces for which responses are currently outstanding and haven't been outstanding too long; any purported response with an unrecognized nonce must be bogus.

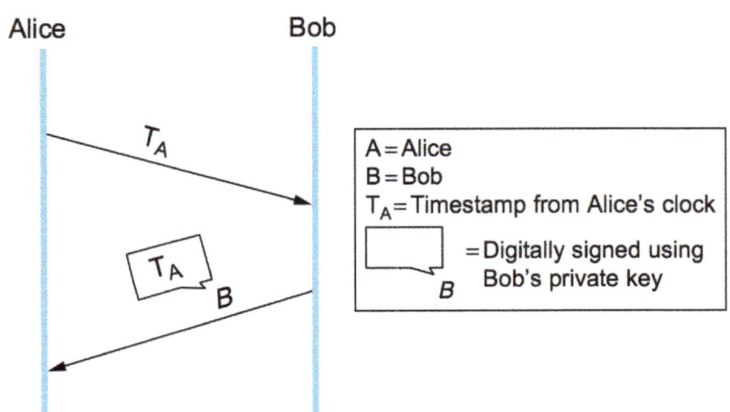

Figure 7: A challenge-response protocol.

The beauty of challenge-response is that it combines timeliness and authentication; after all, only Bob (and possibly Alice, if it's a secret-key cipher) knows the key necessary to encrypt the never-before-seen timestamp or nonce. Timestamps or nonces are used in most of the authentication protocols that follow.

5.2 Public-Key Authentication Protocols

In the following discussion, we assume that Alice and Bob's public keys have been predistributed to each other via some means as described in the previous chapter. This could include the case where Alice includes her certificate in her first message to Bob, and the case where Bob searches some sort of public key infrastructure for a certificate about Alice when he receives her first message.

We describe here a simple authentication protocol that uses timestamps, illustrated in Figure 8. In this protocol, Alice sends Bob a digitally signed message with a timestamp from her local clock and her identity. Because their clocks aren't synchronized, Bob cannot be sure that the message is fresh. Bob sends back a digitally signed message with Alice's original timestamp, his own locally generated timestamp, and his identity. Alice can verify the freshness of Bob's reply by comparing her current time against the timestamp that originated with her. She then sends Bob a digitally signed message with his original timestamp and a new session key encrypted using Bob's public key. Bob can verify the freshness of the message because the timestamp came from his clock, so he knows he can trust the new session key.

The timestamps in this example essentially serve as convenient nonces, and indeed this protocol could use nonces instead. We will see some examples of this when we look at Transport Layer Security (TLS) in a later chapter.

5.3 Secret-Key Authentication Protocols

Only in fairly small systems is it practical to predistribute secret keys to every pair of entities. We focus here on larger systems, where each entity would have its own *master key* shared only with a Key Distribution Center (KDC). In this case, secret-key-based authentication protocols involve three parties: Alice, Bob, and a KDC. The end product of the authentication protocol is a session key shared between Alice and Bob that they will use to communicate directly, without involving the KDC.

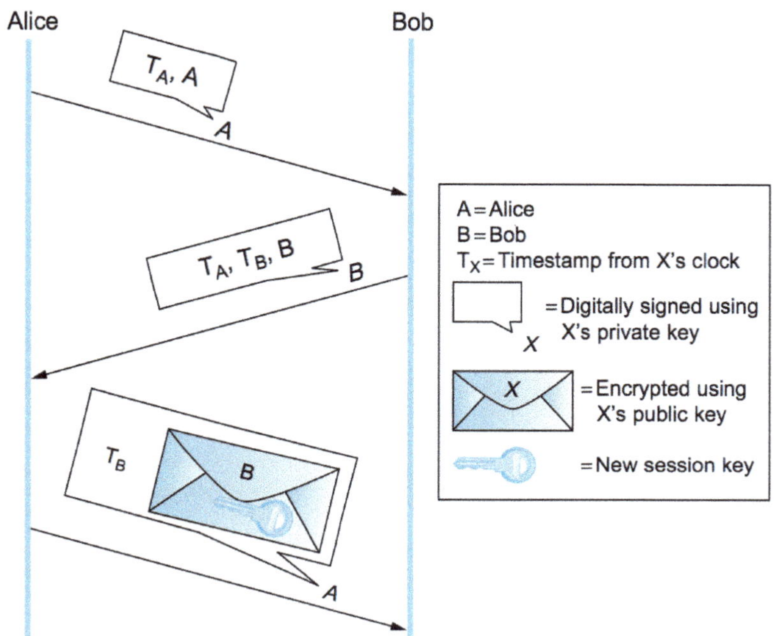

Figure 8: A public-key authentication protocol. Alice checks her own timestamp, signed by Bob, against her own clock, and Bob does the same with his timestamp signed by Alice.

The Needham-Schroeder authentication protocol formed the basis for many future authentication systems, and is illustrated in Figure 9. Note that the KDC doesn't actually authenticate Alice's initial message and doesn't communicate with Bob at all. Instead, the KDC uses its knowledge of Alice's and Bob's master keys to construct a reply that would be useless to anyone other than Alice (because only Alice can decrypt it) and contains the necessary ingredients for Alice and Bob to perform the rest of the authentication protocol themselves.

The process begins with Alice sending a message to the KDC that includes a nonce and the names of the two principals, A(lice) and B(ob). The KDC responds by creating a new session key, encrypting that with the key that the KDC shares with Bob (indicated by the small, inner envelope), and including that in a message sent back to Alice. This message is in turn encrypted using the key that is shared by the KDC and Alice (as indicated by the outer envelope). Thus, only Alice can decrypt this message, and now she has both the unencrypted session key and an encrypted copy of the session key to

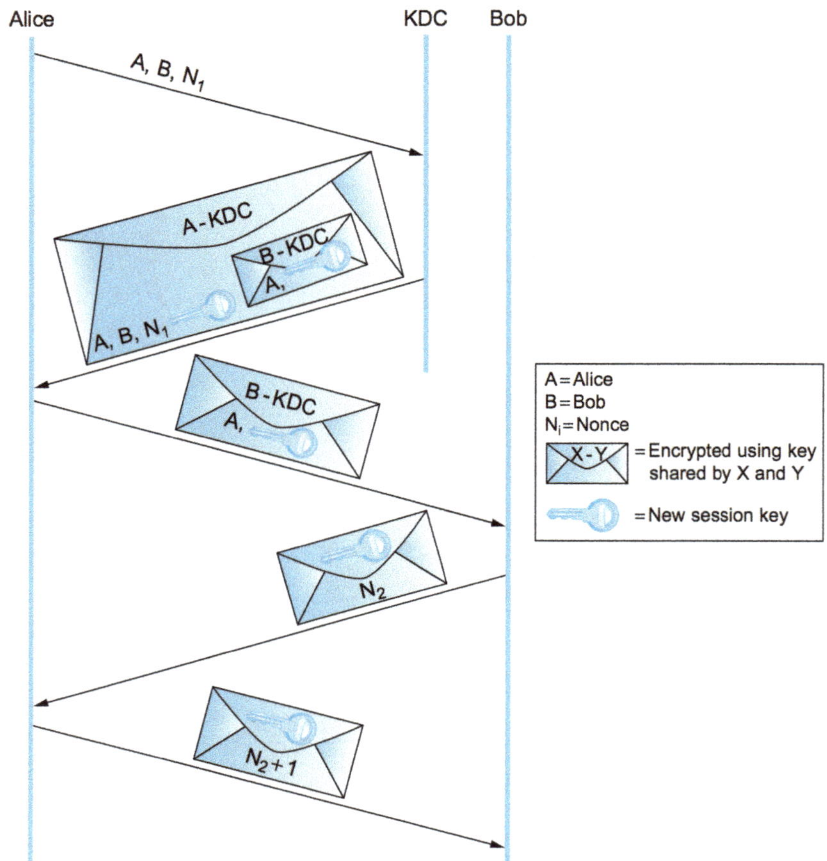

Figure 9: The Needham-Schroeder authentication protocol.

send to Bob. On receiving the message from Alice, Bob is able to decrypt it and obtain the session key. He now creates another nonce and encrypts it with the session key and replies to Alice. Finally, Alice decrypts the nonce, increments it, and replies to Bob with the encrypted result, proving that she has seen the nonce. Although the nonce created by Bob and used in the last two messages shows that the final message from Alice is fresh, it does not guarantee freshness of the initial message Bob received from Alice at step 3. Kerberos addresses this shortcoming.

5.3.1 Kerberos

Kerberos is an authentication system based on the Needham-Schroeder protocol and specialized for client/server environments. Originally developed at MIT, it has been standardized by the IETF and is available as both open source and commercial products. We focus here on some of Kerberos's interesting innovations. Notably, it addresses the freshness problem identified in Needham-Schroeder by using timestamps rather than nonces.

Kerberos clients are generally human users, and users authenticate themselves using passwords. Alice's master key, shared with the KDC, is derived from her password—if you know the password, you can compute the key. Kerberos assumes anyone can physically access any client machine; therefore, it is important to minimize the exposure of Alice's password or master key not just in the network but also on any machine where she logs in. Kerberos takes advantage of an approach derived from Needham-Schroeder to accomplish this. In Needham-Schroeder, the only time Alice needs to use her password to access her master key is when decrypting the reply from the KDC. Kerberos client-side software waits until the KDC's reply arrives, prompts Alice to enter her password, computes the master key and decrypts the KDC's reply, and then erases all information about the password and master key to minimize its exposure. Also note that the only sign a user sees of Kerberos is when the user is prompted for a password.

In Needham-Schroeder, the KDC's reply to Alice plays two roles: It gives her the means to prove her identity (only Alice can decrypt the reply), and it gives her a sort of secret-key certificate or "ticket" to present to Bob—the session key and Alice's identifier, encrypted with Bob's master key. In Kerberos, those two functions—and the KDC itself, in effect—are split up (Figure 10). A trusted server called an Authentication Server (AS) plays the first KDC role of providing Alice with something she can use to prove her identity—not to Bob this time, but to a second trusted server called a Ticket Granting Server (TGS). The TGS plays the second KDC role, replying to Alice with a ticket she can present to Bob. The attraction of this scheme is that if Alice needs to communicate with several servers, not just Bob, then she can get tickets for each of them from the TGS without going back to the AS.

Once Alice has received the ticket from the AS, she is able to communicate with the TGS. She provides the ticket, the identifier for Bob, and an encrypted timestamp (in place of the nonce used in Needham-Schroeder). The TGS replies with a ticket that will be readable by Bob, because it is encrypted with his master key, and a session key that is encrypted using the key shared by Alice and the TGS. Alice can now start communicating with Bob, sending the ticket and another encrypted timestamp using the newly provided session key.

In the client/server application domain for which Kerberos is intended, it is reasonable to assume a degree of clock synchronization. This allows Kerberos to use timestamps and lifespans instead of Needham-Shroeder's nonces. This means that the TGS and Bob can both be assured that the messages that came from Alice are fresh and not replays, thereby eliminating the Needham-Schroeder security weakness noted above. The freshness of Bob's reply to Alice is assured because it is a response to the challenge from Alice.

Kerberos has undergone considerable development and standardization over the decades. It supports a choice of hash functions and secret-key ciphers, which has allowed it to evolve along with the standards for cryptographic algorithms.

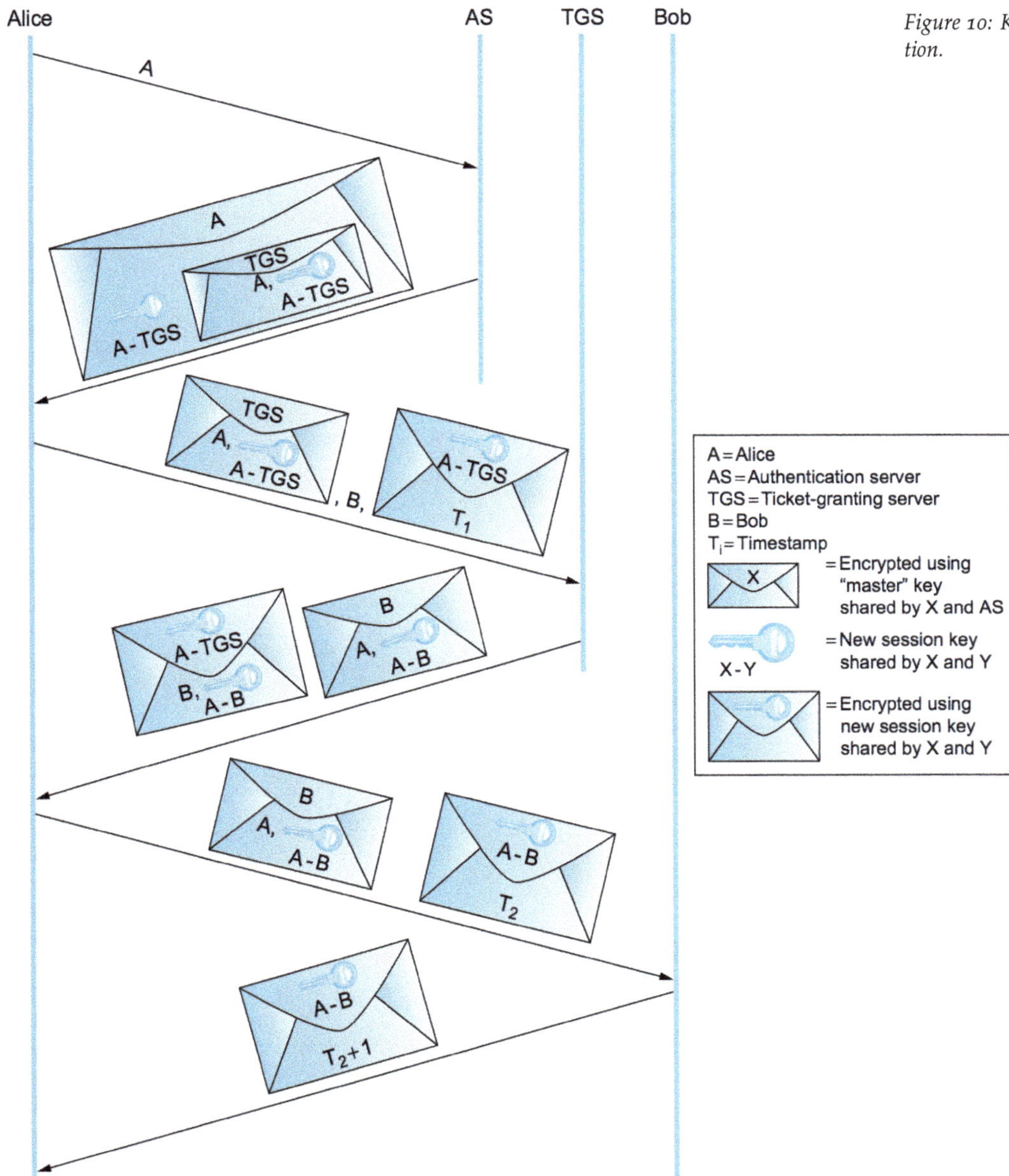

Figure 10: Kerberos authentication.

Chapter 6. Transport Security

To understand the design goals and requirements for the Transport Layer Security (TLS) standard and the Secure Socket Layer (SSL) on which TLS is based, it is helpful to consider the main problems that they were invented to solve. As the World Wide Web became popular and commercial enterprises began to take an interest in it, it became clear that some level of security would be necessary for transactions on the Web. The canonical example of this is making purchases by credit card. There are several issues of concern when sending your credit card information to a computer on the Web. First, you might worry that the information would be intercepted in transit and subsequently used to make unauthorized purchases. You might also worry about the details of a transaction being modified, such as changing the purchase amount. And you would certainly like to know that the computer to which you are sending your credit card information is in fact one belonging to the vendor in question and not some other party. Thus, we immediately see a need for confidentiality, integrity, and authentication in Web transactions. The first widely used solution to this problem was SSL, originally developed by Netscape and subsequently the basis for the IETF's TLS standard.

The designers of SSL and TLS recognized that these problems were not specific to Web transactions (i.e., those using HTTP) and thus they built a general-purpose protocol that sits between an application protocol such as HTTP and a transport protocol such as TCP. The reason for calling this "transport layer security" is that, from the application's perspective, this protocol layer looks just like a normal transport protocol except for the fact that it is secure. That is, the sender can open connections and deliver bytes for transmission, and the secure transport layer will get them to the receiver with the necessary confidentiality, integrity, and authentication. By running the secure transport layer on top of TCP, all of the normal features of TCP (reliability, flow control, congestion control, etc.) are also provided to the application. This arrangement of protocol layers is depicted in Figure 11.

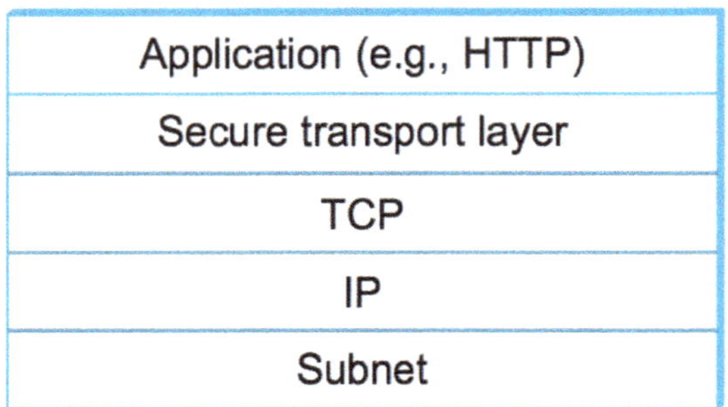

Figure 11: Secure transport layer inserted between application and TCP layers.

When HTTP is used in this way, it is known as HTTPS (Secure HTTP). In fact, HTTP itself is unchanged. It simply delivers data to and accepts data from the SSL/TLS layer rather than TCP. For convenience, a default TCP port has been assigned to HTTPS (443). That is, if you try to connect to a server on TCP port 443, you will likely find yourself talking to the SSL/TLS protocol, which will pass your data through to HTTP provided all goes well with authentication and decryption. Although standalone implementations of SSL/TLS are available, it is more common for an implementation to be bundled with applications that need it, primarily web browsers and servers.

The layered approach, inserting TLS between the application protocol and the transport protocol, is not without drawbacks, particularly when performance is considered. This eventually led to a rethinking of the layering and a new transport protocol, QUIC, was developed with the benefit of decades of experience with TLS and HTTP. We return to this development below.

The following discussion focuses on TLS, as SSL is now a historical artifact. TLS continues to evolve as new weaknesses are identified and fixed, and new cryptographic algorithms continue to be added, often replacing older ones now considered insufficiently strong.

Like TCP, TLS has a setup phase involving handshakes followed by a connected phase in which data is exchanged between the endpoints. We discuss each in turn, beginning with the *handshake protocol* that supports initial setup. Once the connection properties are established by the handshake, the *record protocol* is used to protect the data sent between the endpoints.

Performance is always important when applying cryptographic operations to data transfers, and it has a significant impact on end-to-end latency for web interactions. One performance-related design choice is the use of symmetric key cryptography for the encryption and authentication of data after the handshake is complete. In addition, there have been efforts to reduce the number of round-trip times required to begin data transfer, thus lowering initial latency. We examine these developments later in this chapter.

6.1 Handshake Protocol

The main job of the handshake protocol is to allow a pair of TLS participants to establish a shared secret key and negotiate at runtime the set of cryptographic algorithms to use. It also allows for version negotiation, so that, for example, a client running TLS version 1.2 can talk to a server that supports both version 1.2 and 1.3. It also allows the client to authenticate the server, and, optionally, for the client to be authenticated as well.

The handshake protocol needs to be resistant to man-in-the-middle (MITM) attacks, which we discussed in Chapter 4. At one point in its history, TLS version negotiation could be subverted by a MITM in such a way that the client and server settled on a lower version than necessary. Such a "downgrade attack" opens up the risk that old vulnerabilities in the lower version, such as weak cryptographic protocols, could be exploited.

TLS takes multiple precautions to increase its resistance against MITM attacks. TLS 1.3 encrypts most of the handshake protocol, as early in the process as possible. To facilitate this, the first step of the handshake entails the establishment of a shared secret between the client and the server. This is most commonly achieved using an ephemeral Diffie-Hellman key exchange as described in Chapter 4. Pre-shared keys are also supported and have a role in restarting a session quickly, as discussed in Section 6.3.

When we described Diffie-Hellman in chapter 4 we explained the original algorithm that operates on groups of integers using modular arithmetic. This is now known as Finite Field Diffie-Hellman. It is also possible to use elliptic curves rather than modular arithmetic and both options are available in modern TLS.

There are a number of ways the handshake protocol can play out, but a typical set of operations is as follows:

1. The client sends a "client hello" message which specifies which Diffie-Hellman groups or elliptic curves it supports, along with an ephemeral Diffie-Hellman key for each group/curve. The hello also contains a nonce, the set of cipher suites that the client can use for subsequent encryption and authentication, and the TLS version the client supports.

2. The server replies with a "server hello" message indicating which Diffie-Hellman group or curve it has chosen and a corresponding ephemeral Diffie-Hellman public key. The hello also states which TLS version the server supports, the cipher suite it has chosen among those offered by the client, and a nonce.

Recall that a simple Diffie-Hellman key exchange is not secure against MITM attacks, and the remaining steps in the handshake protect against this. From the first two messages, the server and the client are able to agree on a shared secret using one of several Diffie-Hellman algorithms. A choice of groups or curves were provided in the client hello, and one of them has been selected by the server. Similarly, one of the offered cipher suites has been selected. With Diffie-Hellman allowing them to obtain a shared secret, all subsequent messages between client and server will be encrypted. But we still have to rule out the MITM attack.

3. The server now sends one or more certificates. In the simplest case, there is a single certificate signed by a certificate authority (CA) that is trusted by the client.

4. The server sends a "certificate verify" message, which proves that the server has the private key that corresponds to the public key in the previously supplied certificate. The signature covers everything that has been sent in the handshake up to this point, which includes a pair of nonces, thus providing protection against replay attacks. And the signature along with the certificate is sufficient to prove to the client that it is talking to the intended server, not to some attacker in the middle, who would be unable to provide the signature.

5. The server sends a "handshake finished" message which contains a hash of everything sent so far, ensuring that nothing in the handshake was tampered with. This further protects against MITM attacks.

6. The client sends a similar "handshake finished" message.

At this point the client knows that it is talking to the intended server, and both parties know that they have successfully completed the handshake without any tampering of messages. The server in this case does not know who the client is because there has been no client authentication. TLS does support client authentication using client certificates, but it is not the norm in today's Internet for clients to authenticate in this way.

Recall that public key cryptography is computationally more expensive than symmetric key cryptography, so we limit the use of public key operations to the handshake protocol. And when we said above that all the messages after the first two are encrypted, this is done using symmetric keys. The roles of public keys in TLS are (a) the Diffie-Hellman key exchange (b) the use of certificates to authenticate servers and, optionally, clients. All of that is limited to the handshake protocol.

Figure 12 shows the handshake protocol at a high level. When the client and server have each received a "handshake finished" message from their respective peer, the handshake is complete and application data can start to flow.

Encryption of data between client and server is performed by TLS's *record protocol*. Because the handshake protocol in TLS 1.3 requires

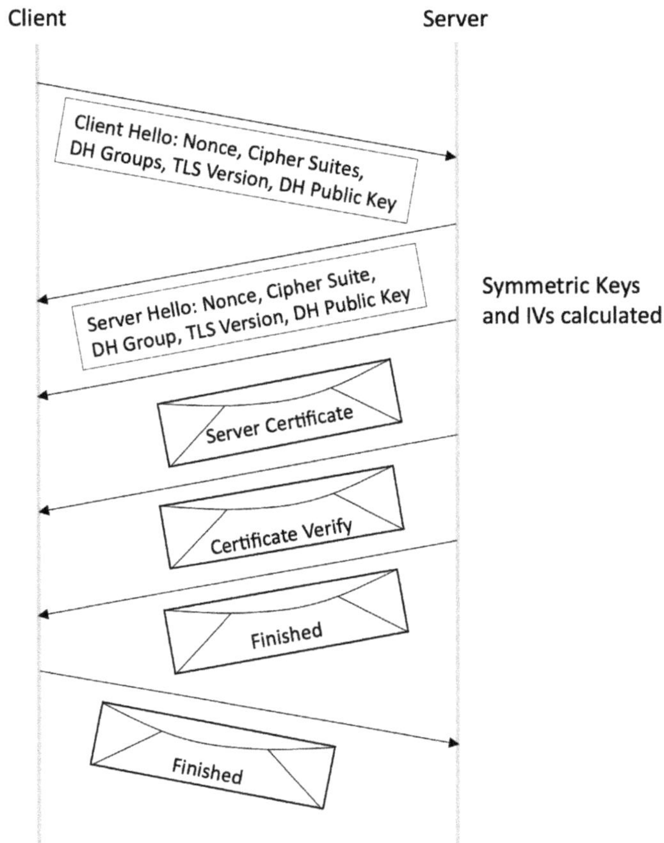

Figure 12: Handshake protocol to establish TLS session.

encryption after the first two messages, the record protocol actually comes into play at step 3 above, even before we get to sending any application data. We discuss the details of the record protocol below.

6.2 Record Protocol

The task of the record protocol is to protect the data that is sent over a TLS connection with both encryption and authentication. While TLS supports a wide range of encryption and authentication methods, the set of options has actually become narrower in version 1.3 as weaknesses of older methods became clear and new cryptographic algorithms have emerged. All the algorithms in TLS 1.3 provide both encryption and authentication in a single cipher suite, using the technique known as authenticated encryption with additional data (AEAD) which was discussed in Chapter 3.

In TLS, the cipher that provides authentication and encryption uses two keys, one for each direction. Similarly, two initialization vectors are required. Thus, regardless of the choice of cipher suite, a TLS session requires effectively four keys to be agreed upon by the end points. TLS derives all of them from a single shared secret that was obtained during the handshake phase.

The step that derives the keys and initialization vectors from the shared secret is called the "HMAC-based extract-and-expand key derivation function (HKDF)". The goal is to produce enough keying material for the record layer–two IVs and two symmetric keys of appropriate length–and to do so in such a way that an attacker has no better way of guessing them than a brute force attack. In other words, we want the keys and IVs to be as close to random as possible. This is a bit harder than it might first appear, because the shared secret that is obtained via Diffie Hellman, which is our starting point, is not itself completely random. The reason for this may not be obvious, but the goal of the various Diffie Hellman algorithms is to generate a shared secret, not that such secrets be randomly distributed.

There is some fairly serious mathematics underlying HKDF, but the basic idea is called "extract and expand". The first step is to "extract" the randomness from the shared secret. This is done by calculating a HMAC (hash-based message authentication code, as described in Chapter 3) over the shared secret. The resulting pseudorandom key is input to the next stage, along with an additional source of randomness: the hash of everything contained in the initial handshake. Note that the handshake messages include two random nonces. The "expand" step then applies the HMAC function using these inputs and HMAC is reapplied as many times as needed to produce the required amount of key and IV material.

When all the keys and IVs are available to client and server, the record layer can now protect the underlying data with encryption and authentication. The record layer also handles fragmentation and reassembly–breaking the incoming stream of plaintext into chunks of up to 2^{14} bytes.

To encrypt one block for transmission, the record layer takes as input the encryption key, a nonce (which we explain below), the plaintext to be encrypted, and "additional data" to be authenticated but not encrypted. This additional data is the header for the record layer, indicating the type of data being encrypted (e.g., application data or handshake data) and its length. The nonce is calculated by computing the XOR of the IV and a sequence number that increments with every block. The AEAD cipher then computes the ciphertext that will follow the record header, and the resulting block is passed to the transport layer (normally TCP) for transmission.

On the receiving side, the process runs in the other direction, with the appropriate key, nonce, ciphertext and additional data (headers) being passed to the AEAD decryption function. If authentication is successful, the plaintext is recovered and can be passed up to the application. If authentication does not succeed, the connection is terminated and an alert is generated.

6.3 Session Resumption and Zero RTT Operation

In our initial description of the TLS handshake, we described how Diffie-Hellman is used to established a shared secret, but noted that the option also exists to use a pre-shared key (PSK). While out-of-band provisioning of a PSK is possible, a much more common use of a PSK is to allow session resumption, thus removing the need to go through another Diffie-Hellman exchange.

An important side-effect of using a pre-shared key is that it becomes possible to start sending data earlier in the process. This operation is referred to as "0-RTT Data" because it is possible to start sending application data along with the handshake material without waiting for the round trip time of the handshake to elapse. This is an important step in improving the latency of HTTPS connection establishment and thus the user experience when browsing the Web.

The idea of session resumption predates TLS 1.3 but it has evolved somewhat to become more secure. In TLS 1.3, the server may create a *session ticket* after the completion of the handshake process. The ticket contains an opaque identifier of the session and a ticket lifetime (as well as some other fields). The ticket is sent after the handshake which means it is encrypted much like application data. More than one ticket can be sent.

A ticket is effectively a label for a previously established session, which has a shared secret already. When a client connects to a server to which it was previously connected, it can look at its stored tickets and, if there are any that have not expired, it can include one in the first message of a handshake. Along with the ticket, the client includes something called a "binding", which is a HMAC calculated over the current handshake message using a key derived from the *previous* handshake. The effect of this binding is to tie the new handshake back to the old one, since only a client that successfully completed the prior handshake can have the key required to calculate the HMAC. Thus, while an attacker might snoop on the ticket, it can't do much with it and any attempt to modify the new handshake message will fail.

When the server sees that the client has sent a ticket, it validates the binding, and if the HMAC calculation succeeds, then the server and client now have agreement that they can use a shared secret established in the prior session. They use a "resumption master secret" that was calculated and stored in the prior session to derive a new set of keys for this session. The keys of the new session are different from those of the prior session to support forward secrecy (i.e., even if an attacker manages to compromise the key for one session, they don't gain the ability to decrypt data from other sessions).

When the server sends its "Finished" message, it calculates the HMAC over the handshake messages using the agreed-upon new key, and thus authenticates itself to the client.

On its own, session resumption as just described may not seem that interesting. It avoids the need for another Diffie-Hellman exchange but is still requires a round trip time to establish the session. But because the new session keys are known to both sides before the first handshake message is sent, session resumption opens up the possibility of sending "0-RTT data" along with the handshake. 0-RTT data can be included along with the handshake messages, without waiting one

RTT for keys to be established. This is beneficial from a performance perspective, especially for short-lived connections, but it comes with some downsides in terms of security.

There are two main drawbacks to 0-RTT data. The first is that it is prone to replay attacks in a way that other data transfers are not. If an attacker can sit between a client and a server, they have the opportunity to replay 0-RTT data. Exactly how much damage this does is very much application dependent, so the TLS specifications dictate that (a) 0-RTT data can only be sent when the application layer explicitly requests it, i.e., it can't just be an optimization provided by the socket layer (b) the application must know how to deal with replays of data sent as 0-RTT, e.g., by only sending 0-RTT data for operations that are idempotent.

The other drawback of 0-RTT data is that it depends on a potentially long-lived secret. The resumption key used to encrypt 0-RTT data is derived from shared key material that was established in an earlier session. This material is retained by the server for some period of time to allow for future resumptions. If that secret were somehow compromised at some point in the future, an attacker who had recorded the 0-RTT data would have the necessary information to decrypt it. Thus, 0-RTT data lacks forward secrecy. For this reason, the option exists to generate a new set of keys as part of the session resumption handshake with a new Diffie-Hellman exchange. This means that only the data sent in the first RTT lacks forward secrecy, and the rest of the session is protected by the new ephemeral keys.

All of this work to reduce the setup time of TLS by a single RTT might seem surprising, but in fact the history of HTTP and HTTPS over TCP is full of issues with excessive setup times. The very first implementations of HTTP were quite wasteful of TCP connections, setting up a new connection for every object on a requested web page. The history of HTTP over TCP and the addition of TLS is full of efforts to reduce the latency since the most simple approaches just layered one handshake on top of another. The next step in the process of reducing the latency of TLS session establishment involves rethinking the choice of TCP as the underlying transport, as we discuss below.

6.4 QUIC, HTTP/3 and TLS

Since the invention of the World Wide Web in the 1990s, HTTP has run over TCP. HTTP/1.0, the original version, had quite a number of performance problems due to the way it used TCP, such as the fact that every request for an object required a new TCP connection to be set up and then closed after the reply was returned. HTTP/1.1 was proposed at an early stage to make better use of TCP. TCP continued to be the protocol used by HTTP for another twenty-plus years.

Adding security to HTTP-over-TCP in the form of SSL and TLS further exacerbated performance issues, even as advancements to HTTP mitigated some of the original problems. As noted in the preceding section, it takes at least one round trip time to establish a secure TLS session. The relatively recent introduction of 0-RTT data reduces the latency before the first data can be sent; it also comes with some security drawbacks as we observed above.

Of course, the time required to set up a secure session with TLS in *in addition* to the time need to set up a TCP connection. TCP needs to complete its 3-way handshake before the first TLS handshake message-which is just data as far as TCP is concerned-can be sent. So the sequence of events was:

- Client initiates TCP 3-way handshake to establish TCP session.
- TLS handshake establishes security parameters for client-server communication.
- First HTTP message gets sent from client to server.

In other words, in the original TLS-over-TCP model it would take at least three RTTs to get a response to a single HTTPS request. In fact up until TLS 1.3 arrived it was at least four RTTs due to the use of two RTTs to complete the TLS handshake.

This is not the only problem with running HTTP over TCP. A reliable, ordered byte stream as provided by TCP isn't exactly the right model for Web traffic. In particular, since most web pages contain many objects, it makes sense to be able to request many objects in parallel, but TCP only provides a single byte stream. If one packet is lost,

TCP waits for its retransmission and successful delivery before continuing, while HTTP would have been happy to receive other objects that were not affected by that single lost packet. Opening multiple TCP connections would appear to be a solution to this, but that has its own set of drawbacks including a lack of shared information about congestion across connections.

Other factors such as the rise of high-latency wireless networks and the availability of multiple networks for a single device (e.g., Wi-Fi and cellular) contributed to the realization that the transport layer for HTTP would benefit from a new approach. The protocol that emerged to fill this need was QUIC.

In this section we will focus on how QUIC particularly improves the performance of TLS compared to running over TCP. QUIC is quite a comprehensive re-working of the transport layer that could fill its own book-indeed the set of RFCs that define it run to the hundreds of pages.

QUIC originated at Google in 2012 and was subsequently developed as a proposed standard at the IETF. It has already seen a solid amount of deployment—it is in most Web browsers, many popular websites, and is even starting to be used for non-HTTP applications. Deployability was a key consideration for the designers of the protocol. There are a lot of moving parts to QUIC—its specification spans three RFCs—but we focus here on how it changes the relationship between TLS and the underlying transport.

The single most important change in QUIC from the perspective of TLS performance is that it doesn't treat the transport and security handshakes as two distinct layers. Instead, QUIC has build a cryptographic handshake based on TLS into the transport. This is illustrated by Figure foo. As RFC 9001 puts it:

> *Rather than a strict layering, these two protocols cooperate: QUIC uses the TLS handshake; TLS uses the reliability, ordered delivery, and record layer provided by QUIC.*

This rearrangement of layers takes a bit of work to understand. The central idea is that QUIC has the ability to provide encryption and authentication to the data it transmits once it has a set of keys

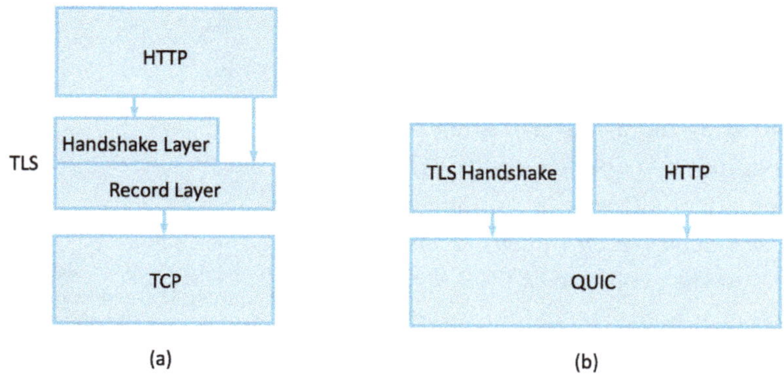

Figure 13: Protocol stacks compared. (a) HTTP over TLS over TCP. (b) HTTP and TLS Handshake over QUIC.

to work with. So the TLS handshake operates pretty much as it did over TCP, but instead of wrapping up TLS handshake messages in the TLS record layer before sending them out over TCP, we can send the TLS handshake messages over QUIC directly. QUIC also provides the reliability, congestion control, etc. that TCP provides. Once the TLS handshake is complete, the keying material for the connection is passed to QUIC, which now is able to encrypt and authenticate the data that is sent by HTTP.

The most obvious practical impact of this is that the establishment of a QUIC connection takes place at the same time as the transmission of TLS handshake messages, rather than taking place prior to the TLS handshake as with TCP. By the time the TLS handshake completes, the two ends of the QUIC connection have all the state needed to transmit data such as HTTP messages. Furthermore, in the cases where 0-RTT data can be sent (because there are shared secrets cached from a previous connection), the first HTTP request can actually be sent at the same time as the client Hello message.

A final detail of note is that QUIC runs on top of UDP rather than directly over IP. The reason behind this is that there are plenty of middleboxes in the Internet that assume that the only acceptable transport protocols are TCP and UDP and block anything else. So while UDP doesn't add much in the way of useful functionality to QUIC, it was an expedient step to run QUIC over UDP to ease deployment of QUIC in the Internet.

QUIC is an interesting development in the world of transport protocols and not just for its impact on security. Many of the limitations of TCP have been known for decades, but QUIC represents one of the most successful efforts to date to stake out a different point in the design space. Because QUIC was inspired by experience with HTTP, TLS, and the Web—which arose long after TCP was well established in the Internet—it presents a fascinating case study in the unforeseen consequences of layered designs and in the evolution of the Internet. There is a lot more to it that we can cover here. The definitive reference for QUIC is RFC 9000, while RFC 9001 covers the relationship of TLS to QUIC. A more readable overview of the protocol's design and deployment appears in a paper from SIGCOMM 2017.

Further Reading:

A. Langley *et al.* The QUIC Transport Protocol: Design and Internet-Scale Deployment. Proc. ACM SIGCOMM, August 2017.

L. Peterson, L. Brakmo, and B. Davie, TCP Congestion Control: A Systems Approach.

6.5 A Systems View of TLS

When we talk about "The Systems Approach", we always come back to the need to consider how all the parts of a system interact with each other to form a coherent whole, rather than just looking at single components in isolation. For example, TLS is a system that includes both public-key and symmetric-key cryptography, authentication and privacy mechanisms, certificate authorities, and sub-layers such as the record protocol and the handshake protocol. But the systems approach applies recursively too. As we have already seen, it is important to look at how TLS sits within the overall protocol stack, with HTTP and other applications above it, and a choice of transport layer protocols (TCP and QUIC) below it. The interactions among these layers have proven critical to the performance of the World Wide Web and other applications that run over HTTPS.

We can take yet another step back and consider a broader system that includes end users, their browsers, and the servers that make up the World Wide Web. For most users, the only indication that TLS is being used when they browse the Web is a little padlock icon next to the URL in the browser's address bar. Over the decades that SSL and TLS have been in use, the browser companies have, with some success, educated users to expect encrypted connections to most web sites, particularly when data is being sent by the user. If a user tries to send data (e.g., by filling out a form) over an unencrypted HTTP connection, the browser pops up a warning about the risk of doing so. If a certificate has expired or does not match the URL of the site being browsed, another warning is presented. Users can generally choose to override these warnings but the overall effect is to reinforce behaviors that are more secure and discourage those that are insecure.

Certificate authorities are a critical part of this overall system. Most users have no way to determine whether any given CA does its job properly. As discussed in Chapter 4, the way that CA hierarchies work means that a lot of trust is placed at the top-level CAs. These are the CAs that are trusted by default in browsers; if they trust lower-level CAs that are not doing a good job of verifying the legitimacy of organizations to whom they issue certificates, it creates weaknesses in the overall CA system that can be exploited.

An important development in the deployment of TLS was the creation of Let's Encrypt, a CA run by a non-profit that provides TLS certificates at no charge. By making certificates free for web sites, Let's Encrypt helped advance the cause of making encrypted connections on the Web the default. Prior to the establishment of Let's Encrypt, it was typical for sites to pay for a certificate from a CA, and the cost was non-trivial for small sites. Let's Encrypt issues *domain-validated certificates*. Issuance of these certificates can be fully automated and depends on the domain implementing a challenge-response protocol known as ACME (Automated Certificate Management Environment). We won't dwell on the details here, but the availability of certificates that are both free and automatically issued and renewed has dramatically increased the adoption of HTTPS. This in turn helps with setting user expectations that a padlock should be present in their browser's address bar, even if they have no understanding of what is going on under the covers. More detail on Let's Encrypt can be found in the a SIGSAC 2019 paper.

Further Reading:

J. Aas *et al.* Let's Encrypt: An Automated Certificate Authority to Encrypt the Entire Web. SIGSAC 2019.

One area that remains challenging for end users is the ability of malicious actors to create sites that look legitimate and use URLs that are similar enough to the original to fool users. This might be done using easily missed spelling errors (accoounts-google.com being one infamous example). An encrypted connection is of no value to the end user if they are being connected to a malicious site. In Chapter 9 we take a look at passkeys as part of the solution to the problem of phishing attacks that steer users to such sites. Again, the system that we are trying to protect is more than just a connection from a browser to a web site.

One conclusion to draw from this discussion is that we need to take a broad view of the "systems" that we are trying to secure, and the way that users interact with the system are critical to its success. It's also worth recalling some of the points from earlier in the book: any analysis of security should start by looking at the threats that we need to protect against. And there are always going to be trade-offs between the costs we are willing to pay and the security we can provide. TLS is not a perfect of complete solution but it has certainly done a lot to improve security of communication on the Internet.

Chapter 7. Subsystem Security

Having focused on how to use the available cryptographic and authentication building blocks to secure the transport layer—to the benefit of all applications—we now turn our attention to examples of how individual subsystems are secured. The examples address specific threats—associated with specific use cases—that remain even when TLS is deployed.

The systems described in this chapter are at different layers: some are are built into applications, some run at the IP layer, and some secure network links. While they address different layer-specific threats, what the examples have in common is that they all leverage the same set of security building blocks. Seeing how these building blocks can be assembled in different ways to build different solutions is the main value of this chapter. To this end, the following sections focus on the use case and corresponding threat, with a high-level description of how the system addresses the threat; no new algorithms or fundamental capabilities are required.

It is also noteworthy that in addition to taking advantage of existing building blocks, the example systems are highly configurable. The idea of making a security system algorithm independent is a good one, because you never know when your preferred cryptographic algorithm might be proved to be insufficient for your purposes. Note the analogy to being able to change keys without changing the algorithm; if one of your cryptographic algorithms turns out to be flawed, it would be great if your entire security architecture didn't need an immediate redesign.

7.1 *Pretty Good Privacy*

Pretty Good Privacy (PGP) is an approach to providing authentication, confidentiality, data integrity, and nonrepudiation for email. Originally devised by Phil Zimmerman in 1991, it has evolved into an IETF standard known as OpenPGP. As we saw in Chapter 4, PGP is notable for using a "web of trust" model for distribution of keys rather than a tree-like hierarchy.

The other thing of note about PGP is that it is *not* widely used, in large part because most users elect to trust their email provider (or rather, are not concerned about their email being used for marketing purposes). In contrast, PGP is an option for users that put a premium on privacy and being certain about who they are exchanging messages with. The availability of easy-to-use client software has made that option more viable over time.

PGP's confidentiality and receiver authentication depend on the receiver of a message having a public key that is known to the sender. To provide sender authentication and nonrepudiation, the sender must have a public key that is known by the receiver. These public keys are predistributed using certificates and a web-of-trust PKI. PGP supports RSA and DSS for public key certificates. These certificates may additionally specify which cryptographic algorithms are supported or preferred by the key's owner. The certificates provide bindings between email addresses and public keys.

Consider the following example of PGP being used to provide both sender authentication and confidentiality. Suppose Alice has a message to email to Bob. Alice's PGP application goes through the steps illustrated in Figure 14. First, the message is digitally signed by Alice; MD5, SHA-1, and the SHA-2 family are among the hashes that may be used in the digital signature. Her PGP application then generates a new session key for just this one message; AES and 3DES are among the supported secret-key ciphers. The digitally signed message is encrypted using the session key, then the session key itself is encrypted using Bob's public key and appended to the message. Alice's PGP application reminds her of the level of trust she had previously assigned to Bob's public key, based on the number of certificates she

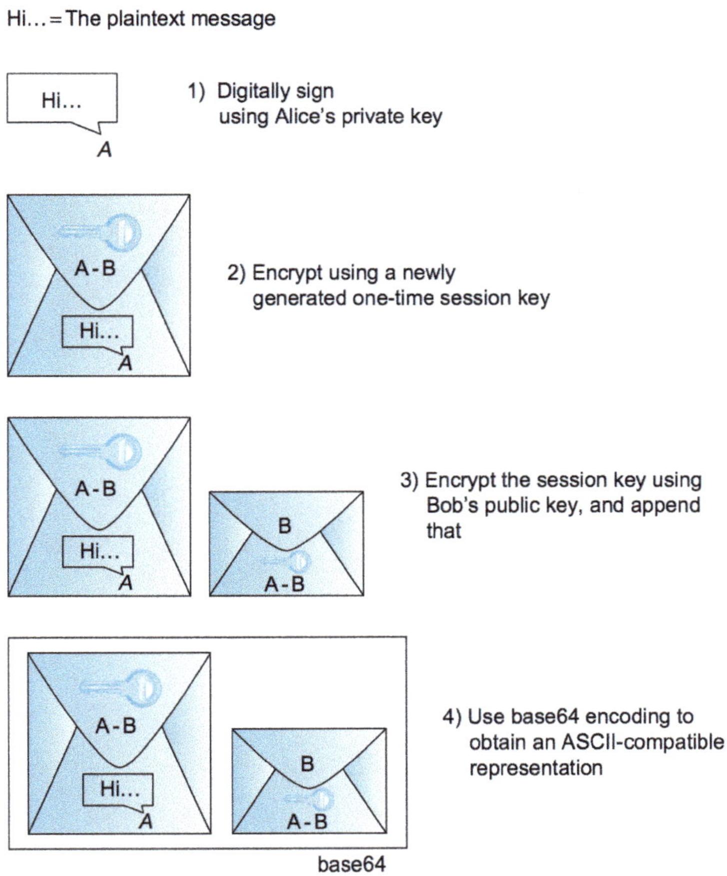

Figure 14: PGP's steps to prepare a message for emailing from Alice to Bob.

has for Bob and the trustworthiness of the individuals who signed the certificates. Finally, not for security but because email messages have to be sent in ASCII, a base64 encoding is applied to the message to convert it to an ASCII-compatible representation. Upon receiving the PGP message in an email, Bob's PGP application reverses this process step-by-step to obtain the original plaintext message and confirm Alice's digital signature—and reminds Bob of the level of trust he has in Alice's public key.

PGP is not strictly for email, but email has particular characteristics that allow PGP to embed an adequate authentication protocol in this one-message data transmission protocol. This avoids the need for any prior message exchange (and sidestepping some of the complexities described in the earlier chapter). Alice's digital signature suffices to authenticate her. Although there is no proof that the message is timely, legitimate email isn't guaranteed to be timely either. There is also no proof that the message is fresh, but Bob is an email user and probably a fault-tolerant human who can recover from duplicate emails (which, again, are not out of the question under normal operation anyway). Alice can be sure that only Bob could read the message because the session key was encrypted with his public key. Although this protocol doesn't prove to Alice that Bob is actually there and received the email, an authenticated email from Bob back to Alice could do this.

The preceding discussion gives a good example of why application-layer security mechanisms can be helpful. Only with a full knowledge of how the application works can you make the right choices about which attacks to defend against (like forged email) versus which to ignore (like delayed or replayed email).

7.2 *Secure Shell*

The Secure Shell (SSH) protocol provides a remote login service, replacing the less secure Telnet used in the early days of the Internet. SSH can also be used to remotely execute commands and transfer files. It is most often used to provide strong client/server authentication and message integrity—where the SSH client runs on the user's laptop (for example) and the SSH server runs on some remote machine that the user wants to log into—but it also supports confidentiality. Telnet provides none of these capabilities. Note that "SSH" is often used to refer to both the SSH protocol and applications that use it; you need to figure out which from the context.

To better appreciate the importance of SSH in today's Internet, consider two scenarios where it is used. Telecommuters depend on some chain of Internet service providers to reach machines operated by their employer. This means that when a telecommuter logs into a machine inside their employer's data center, both the passwords and all the data sent or received potentially passes through any number of untrusted networks. SSH provides a way to encrypt the data sent over these connections and to improve the strength of the authentication mechanism used to log in. (A similar situation occurs when said employee connects to work using the public Wi-Fi at a coffee shop.)

A second common usage of SSH is to login into a remote router, server, or VM for the purpose of managing it; for example, changing its configuration, reading its log files, or installing the latest software. Clearly, administrators want to be sure that they can log into a remote machine securely and that unauthorized parties can neither log in nor intercept the commands sent to the machine or the output sent back to the administrator. This use case is common enough that SSH is often incorporated into more sophisticated management software that automates some aspect of remote operations. This is increasingly the case for tools that support Cloud DevOps, with GitHub, Docker, Ansible, and Jenkins being popular examples that use SSH's remote execution feature.

The latest stable version of SSH, Version 2, consists of three protocols:[3]

- SSH-TRANS, a transport layer protocol
- SSH-AUTH, an authentication protocol
- SSH-CONN, a connection protocol

We focus on the first two, which are involved in remote login. We briefly discuss the purpose of SSH-CONN at the end of the section.

SSH-TRANS provides an encrypted channel between the client and server machines. It runs on top of a TCP connection. Any time a user uses an SSH application to log into a remote machine, the first step is to set up an SSH-TRANS channel between those two machines. The two machines establish this secure channel by first having the client authenticate the server using RSA. Once authenticated, the client and server establish a session key that they will use to encrypt any data sent over the channel. This high-level description skims over several details, including the fact that the SSH-TRANS protocol includes a negotiation of the encryption algorithm the two sides are going to use. For example, AES is commonly selected. Also, SSH-TRANS includes a

[3] Version 3 of SSH (SSH3) has also been proposed, but it is currently an experimental effort that changes the underlying protocols used by SSH. For example, SSH3 runs on top of QUIC (which is UDP-based) instead of TCP. SSH2 remains the widely adopted standard.

message integrity check of all data exchanged over the channel.

The one issue we can't skim over is how the client came to possess the server's public key that it needs to authenticate the server. Strange as it may sound, the server tells the client its public key at connection time. The first time a client connects to a particular server, the SSH application warns the user that it has never talked to this machine before and asks if the user wants to continue. Although it is a risky thing to do, because SSH is effectively not able to authenticate the server, users often say "yes" to this question. This is known as "Trust on First Use" (TOFU). The SSH application then remembers the server's public key; the next time the user connects to that same machine, it compares this saved key with the one the server responds with. If they are the same, SSH authenticates the server. If they are different, however, the SSH application again warns the user that something is amiss, and the user is then given an opportunity to abort the connection.

As an alternative to trust on first use, the prudent user can learn the server's public key through some out-of-band mechanism, save it on the client machine, and thus never take the "first time" risk. As an example, there is an option to publish SSH public key fingerprints in DNS, which then raises the issue of trusting DNS; we return to this topic in Chapter 8.

Once the SSH-TRANS channel exists, the next step is for the user to actually log into the machine, or more specifically, authenticate the user to the server. SSH allows three different mechanisms for doing this. First, since the two machines are communicating over a secure channel, it is OK for the user to simply send their password to the server. This is not a safe thing to do when using Telnet since the password would be sent in the clear, but in the case of SSH, the password is encrypted in the SSH-TRANS channel. The second mechanism uses public-key encryption. This requires that the user has already placed their public key on the server. The third mechanism, called *host-based authentication*, basically says that any user claiming to be so-and-so from a certain set of trusted hosts is automatically believed to be that same user on the server. Host-based authentication requires that the client *host* authenticate itself to the server when the client first connects; standard SSH-TRANS only authenticates the server by default.

The main thing you should take away from this discussion is that SSH is a fairly straightforward application of the protocols and algorithms we have seen throughout this book. However, what sometimes makes SSH a challenge to understand is all the keys a user has to create and manage, where the exact interface is operating system dependent. For example, the OpenSSH package that runs on most Unix machines (e.g., Linux, MacOS) supports a command (ssh-keygen) that can be used to create public/private key pairs. These keys are then stored in various files in directory in the user's home directory. For example, file ~/.ssh/known_hosts records the keys for all the hosts the user has logged into, file ~/.ssh/authorized_keys contains the public keys needed to authenticate the user when logging into this machine (i.e., they are used on the server side). The private keys needed to authenticate the user on remote machines (i.e., keys that are used on the client side) are stored in a file whose name depends on the algorithm. For example, an RSA key would be stored in a file ~/.ssh/id_rsa; an ECDSA key would be stored in ~/.ssh/id_edcsa and so on. These files are usually encrypted with a secret passphrase to protect against the possibility of the private key being compromised by an attacker who gains access to the file.

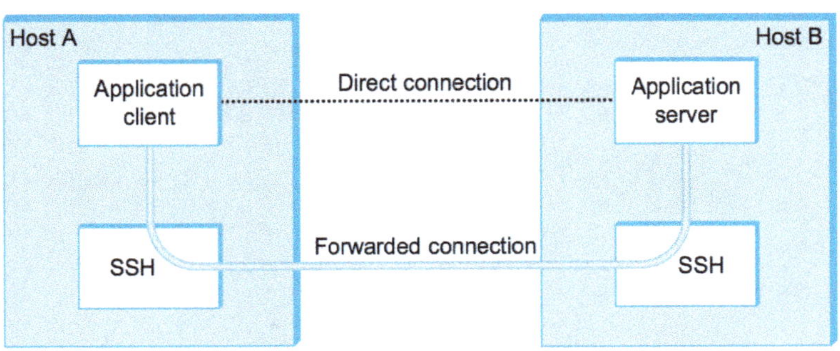

Figure 15: Using SSH port forwarding to secure other TCP-based applications.

Finally, SSH has proven so useful for securing remote login that it has been extended to also support other applications (e.g., sending and receiving email). The idea is to run the applications over a secure "SSH tunnel." This capability is called *port forwarding*, and it uses the SSH-CONN protocol. The idea is illustrated in Figure 15, where we see a client on host A indirectly communicating with a server on host B by forwarding its traffic through an SSH connection. The mechanism is called *port forwarding* because when messages arrive at the well-known SSH port on the server, SSH first decrypts the contents and then "forwards" the data to the actual port at which the server is listening.

Port forwarding effectively creates a secure tunnel that provides confidentiality and authentication. It is possible to provide a kind of virtual private network (VPN) using SSH tunnels in this way, but unlike the VPN mechanism described in the next section, SSH tunnels to a single remote machine rather than to a remote network. The latter gives you access to *any* machine on the local network. In practice, it is also the case that corporate firewalls often block port 22 (SSH's well-known port), limiting the situations in which SSH works as a VPN-like tunnel.

7.3 IP Security

One of the earliest efforts to integrate security into the Internet sits at the IP layer. Support for IPsec, as the architecture is called, is optional in IPv4 but mandatory in IPv6. Indeed, better security was one of the stated goals of IPv6, although it turned out that the central ideas could also be retrofitted into IPv4. It's also noteworthy that while the original intent was for IPsec to be part of securing the network infrastructure (as discussed in the next chapter), today IPsec is most commonly used to implement secure tunnels running on top of the public Internet. These tunnels are often part of a Virtual Private Network (VPN), for example, connecting a remote user to their "home" enterprise network. We turn our attention to VPNs in the next section.

IPsec is really a framework (as opposed to a single protocol or system) for providing a broad set of security services. It provides three degrees of freedom. First, it is highly modular, allowing users (or more likely, system administrators) to select from a variety of cryptographic algorithms and specialized security protocols. Second, IPsec allows users to select from a large menu of security properties, including access control, integrity, authentication, freshness, and confidentiality. Third, IPsec can be used to protect narrow streams (e.g., packets belonging to a particular TCP connection being sent between a pair of hosts) or wide streams (e.g., all packets flowing between a pair of routers or locations).

When viewed from a high level, IPsec consists of two parts. The first part is a pair of protocols that implement the available security services. They are the Authentication Header (AH), which provides access control, connectionless message integrity, authentication, and antireplay protection, and the Encapsulating Security Payload (ESP), which supports these same services, plus confidentiality. AH is rarely used so we focus on ESP here. The second part is support for key management, which fits under an umbrella protocol known as the Internet Security Association and Key Management Protocol (ISAKMP).

The abstraction that binds these two pieces together is the *security association* (SA). An SA is a simplex (one-way) connection with one or more of the available security properties. Securing a bidirectional communication between a pair of hosts—corresponding to a TCP connection, for example—requires two SAs, one in each direction. Although IP is a connectionless protocol, security depends on connection state information such as keys and sequence numbers. When created, an SA is assigned an ID number called a *security parameters index* (SPI) by the receiving machine. A combination of this SPI and the destination IP addresses uniquely identifies an SA. An ESP header includes the SPI so the receiving host can determine which SA an incoming packet belongs to and, hence, what algorithms and keys to apply to the packet.

SAs are established, negotiated, modified, and deleted using ISAKMP. It defines packet formats for exchanging key generation and authentication data. These formats aren't terribly interesting because they provide a framework only—the exact form of the keys and authentication data depends on the key generation technique, the cipher, and the authentication mechanism that is used. Moreover, ISAKMP does not specify a particular key exchange protocol, although it does suggest the Internet Key Exchange (IKE) as one possibility, and IKE v2 is what is used in practice.

ESP is the protocol used to securely transport data over an established SA. In IPv4, the ESP header follows the IP header; in IPv6, it is an extension header. Its format uses both a header and a trailer, as shown in Figure 16. The SPI field lets the receiving host identify the security association to which the packet belongs. The SeqNum field protects against replay attacks. The packet's PayloadData contains the data described by the NextHdr field. If confidentiality is selected, then the data is encrypted using whatever cipher was associated with the SA. The PadLength field records how much padding was added to the data; padding is sometimes necessary because, for example, the cipher requires the plaintext to be a multiple of a certain number of bytes or to ensure that the resulting ciphertext terminates on a 4-byte boundary. Finally, the AuthenticationData carries the authenticator.

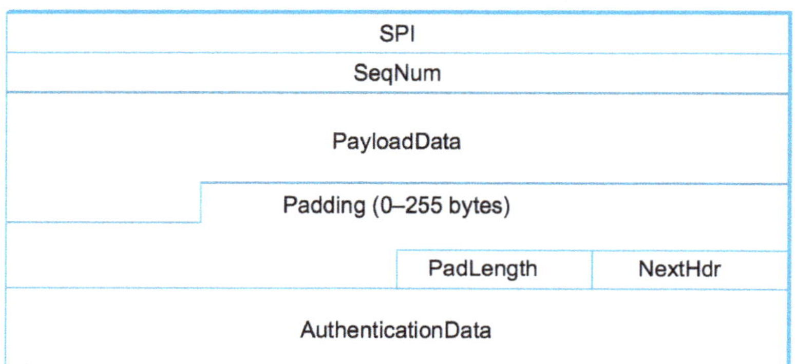

Figure 16: IPSec's ESP format.

IPsec supports a *tunnel mode* as well as the more straightforward *transport mode*. Each SA operates in one or the other mode. In a transport mode SA, ESP's payload data is simply a message for a higher layer such as UDP or TCP. In this mode, IPsec acts as an intermediate protocol layer, much like SSL/TLS does between TCP and a higher layer. When an ESP message is received, its payload is passed to the higher level protocol.

In a tunnel mode SA, however, ESP's payload data is itself an IP packet, as in Figure 17. The source and destination of this inner IP packet may be different from those of the outer IP packet. When an ESP message is received, its payload is forwarded on as a normal IP packet. The most common way to use the ESP is to build an "IPsec tunnel" between two routers, typically firewalls. For example, a corporation wanting to link two sites using the Internet could open a pair of tunnel-mode SAs between a router at one site and a router at the other site. An IP packet outgoing from one site would, at the outgoing router, become the payload of an ESP message sent to the other site's router. The receiving router would unwrap the payload IP packet and forward it on to its true destination.

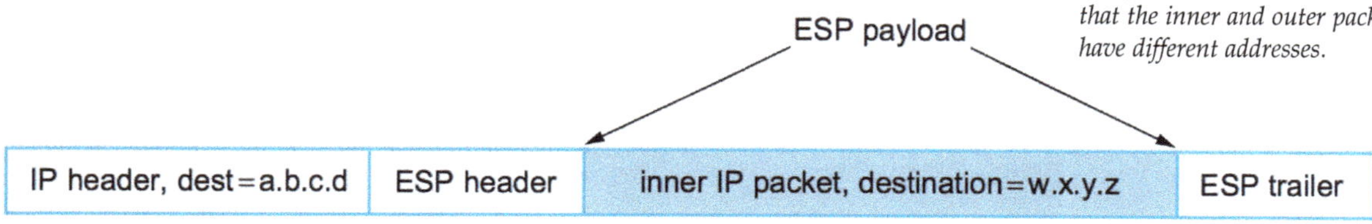

Figure 17: An IP packet with a nested IP packet encapsulated using ESP in tunnel mode. Note that the inner and outer packets have different addresses.

These tunnels may also be configured to use ESP with confidentiality and authentication, thus preventing unauthorized access to the data that traverses this virtual link and ensuring that no spurious data is received at the far end of the tunnel. Furthermore, tunnels can provide traffic confidentiality, since multiplexing multiple flows through a single tunnel obscures information about how much traffic is flowing between particular endpoints. As noted above, a network of such tunnels can be used to implement an entire virtual private network. But there is more to VPNs than just tunneling mechanisms, as we discuss next.

7.4 *Virtual Private Networks*

A virtual private network (VPN) can be built using a wide variety of different technologies, but any VPN requires that we establish connectivity among a set of endpoints. The connections must offer some level of privacy to the principals communicating between those endpoints. Furthermore, to qualify as a *virtual* private network, a VPN creates the illusion of being dedicated to a group of users, even though the underlying infrastructure is shared more widely. In practice, this means that a VPN is almost always built as some sort of overlay on shared infrastructure.

The type of VPN that we focus on here uses tunneling technologies such as IPsec or SSL to provide private connectivity across the shared infrastructure of the Internet. We have already seen how encrypted tunnels can be established, but tunnels are just a building block for VPNs. VPN requirements vary among different use cases, so we begin our discussion by looking at some of the most common uses for VPNs.

Remote Access VPNs are commonly used to support remote workers, telecommuters, or contractors who need access to corporate resources. Figure 18 shows a simple example where a remote user tunnels across the Internet to connect to their corporate office.

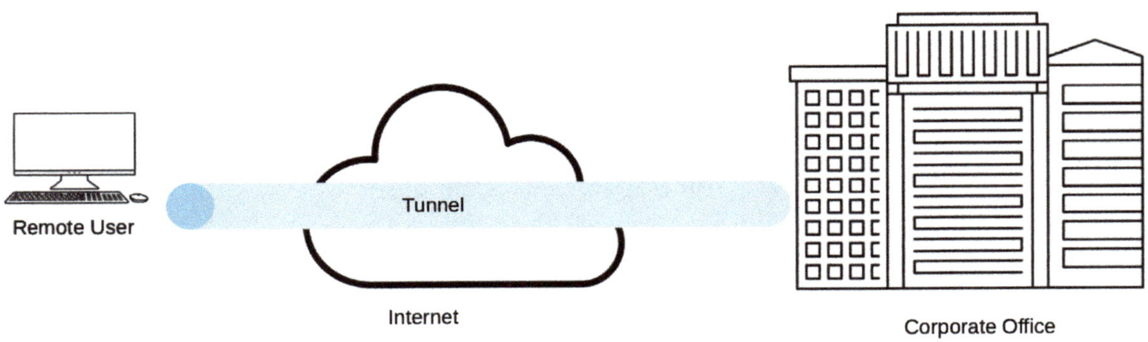

Figure 18: A remote user connects via a tunnel to a corporate site.

Site-to-Site VPNs are generally used to interconnect the sites of an enterprise, which could include datacenters, main corporate offices, and branch offices. Figure 19 shows a simple example for three sites of difference sizes.

Viewed at this level of abstraction, there are obvious similarities between these VPN classes. They are not entirely non-overlapping but they help us identify the requirements. The differences become apparent when we look at the types of devices that terminate tunnels and the methods used to establish them.

Remote access VPNs usually establish tunnels directly from a client device, such as a phone or a laptop, to a device at the edge of the corporate network called a VPN gateway or concentrator. Some VPN client software performs this task, with WireGuard and OpenVPN being two examples of open source, multi-platform clients. There are plenty of proprietary options as well.

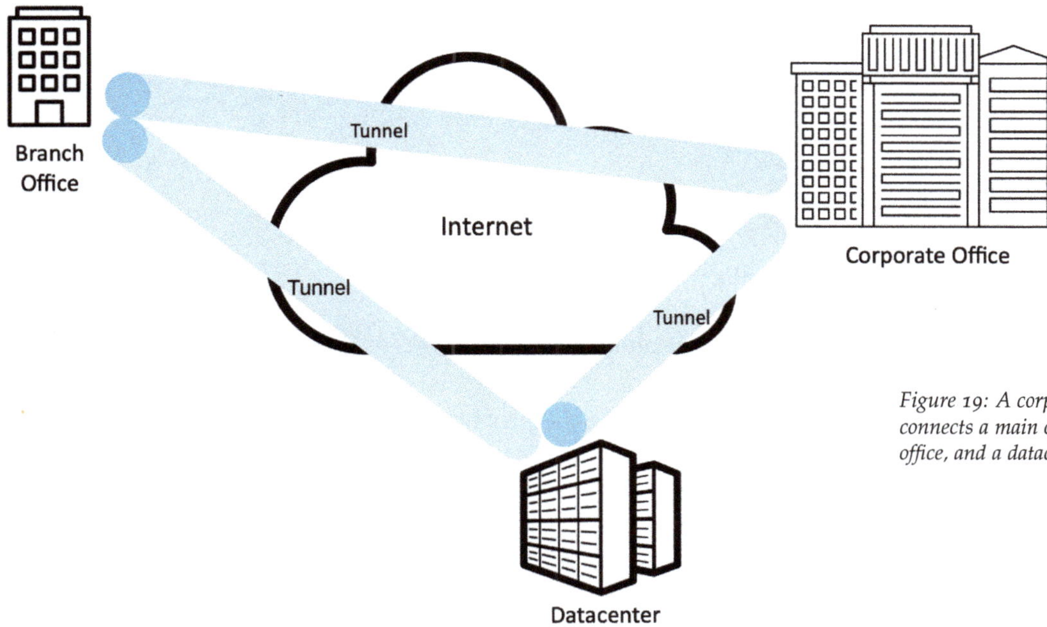

Figure 19: A corporate VPN connects a main office, a branch office, and a datacenter.

OpenVPN leverages TLS to build the encrypted tunnels from client to server. While this mostly follows the same protocol as described in Chapter 6, the additional step of authenticating the client is almost always required in VPN use cases, unlike most Web usages of TLS. Client certificates may be used, but this raises the issue of how certificates can be reliably distributed to client devices. One option is that they are provisioned by a corporate IT department as part of setting up client devices. OpenVPN also allows for other authentication methods, including username plus password and optionally multi-factor authentication.

WireGuard is a more recent implementation of encrypted tunnels that aims to address some shortcomings that have emerged over years of using IPsec and OpenVPN tunnels. The paper below from NDSS 2017 lays out the design philosophy of WireGuard. Compared to OpenVPN, it is less complex by virtue of reducing the set of cryptographic algorithms that it supports. It establishes "stateless" tunnels that are more like IPsec than TLS—that is, there is no transport connection to establish. It also uses the idea of pre-shared public keys for mutual authentication, similar to the approach used in SSH. Finally, it is implemented in the operating system kernel, another contrast to OpenVPN, so as to improve performance. For further details we refer you to the paper.

Further Reading:

J. Donenfeld. WireGuard: Next Generation Kernel Network Tunnel. NDSS, 2017.

One of these types of tunnels plus a gateway or concentrator to terminate them is pretty much all that is needed to deliver a remote access VPN. A concentrator is just an appliance that can handle a large number of VPN tunnels at once, and provides the necessary administrative controls for managing user accounts and interfaces for passing the VPN traffic on to the corporate network. Note that a remote access VPN will almost always have to solve the problem of how to get traffic through the corporate firewall. We cover firewalls in a later chapter, but it is generally the case that VPN traffic is allowed to traverse the firewall so that the VPN user can access corporate resources. The problems of this approach are discussed in the firewalls chapter.

The main difference with site-to-site VPNs is that they aim to connect entire networks together, not just the devices of single remote users. And because office buildings don't move around the way users do, these VPNs are relatively static. Thus, one early approach to building site-to-site VPNs was to simply configure tunnels statically from a router at the edge of one site to a router at the edge of another. Keys could also be statically configured. This would be OK for a small VPN, but as the number of sites increases, the configuration overhead becomes considerable. Furthermore, there is not likely to be an on-site routing and security expert at every branch office, so the configuration would have to be set once before the router was shipped out to the branch and after that point, changes become difficult, especially if the router becomes unreachable for some reason. On top of this, if the connectivity among sites is anything other than a hub and spoke, then the issue of correctly configuring routing protocols to forward traffic across the mesh of tunnels becomes significant.

The complexity of configuring and managing a VPN comprised of encrypted tunnels is one reason why MPLS VPNs, which outsource most of the complexity of VPN management to a service provider, became such a successful service offering in the early 2000s. MPLS does not protect privacy using encryption, but it does solve the issues of routing traffic among large numbers of sites, and with respect to security, ensures that the traffic belonging to one customer does not leak to the network of another. Said another way, MPLS isolates users (private networks) from each other, but users trust that the service provider does not snoop on the traffic they carry. This is a trust assumption that typically does not hold for a VPN that traverses the public Internet.

Several approaches to reduce the configuration overhead for VPNs using encrypted tunnels have appeared in recent years. With the rise of software-defined networking in the 2010s, several companies hit on the idea of using a centralized SDN controller to manage the configuration challenges outlined above. This approach, known as SD-WAN, became one of the successful commercial applications of SDN.

7.4.1 Software-Defined WANs

Provisioning a VPN using MPLS, while less complex than most earlier options, still requires some significant local configuration of both the Customer Edge (CE) router located at each customer site, and the Provider Edge (PE) router to which that site would be connected. In addition, it would typically require the provisioning of a circuit from the customer site to the nearest point of presence for the appropriate Telco.

With SD-WAN, the assumption is that every branch and head office has connectivity to the Internet. An edge router is deployed at each site, and a centralized control plane is used to simplify configuration. An enterprise wants its sites—and only its authorized sites—to be interconnected by the VPN, and it typically wants to apply a set of policies regarding security, traffic prioritization, access to shared services, and so on. These policies are input to a central controller, which can then push out all the necessary configuration to the edge router located at the appropriate office. Rather than manually configuring a router or (multiple routers) every time a new site is added, or configuring tunnels by hand, it is possible to achieve "zero-touch" provisioning: an appliance is shipped to the new site with nothing more than a certificate and an address to contact, which it then uses to contact the central controller and obtain all the configuration it needs. Anything that is necessary to build site-to-site tunnels—IP addresses, routing configuration, secrets, etc.—can be pushed out from the central controller to the edge router. Changes to configuration or policies, which might affect many sites, are input centrally and pushed out to all affected sites. The idea is illustrated in Figure 20.

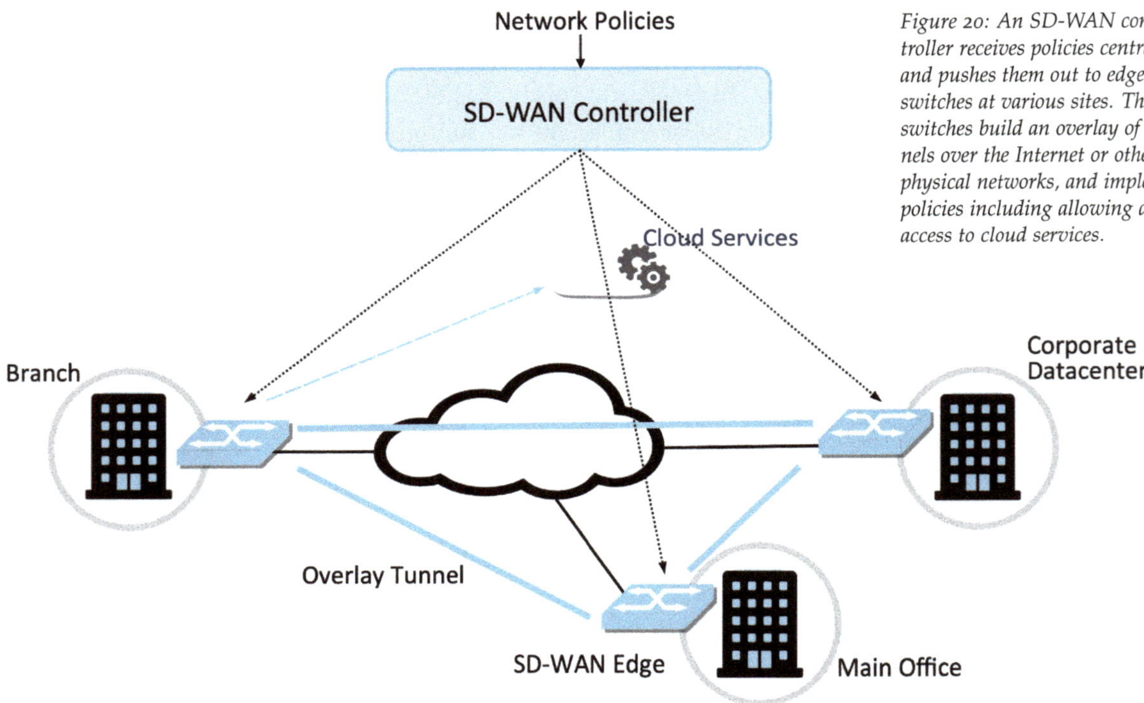

Figure 20: An SD-WAN controller receives policies centrally and pushes them out to edge switches at various sites. The switches build an overlay of tunnels over the Internet or other physical networks, and implement policies including allowing direct access to cloud services.

It can be hard to determine exactly what properties of SD-WAN have made it popular, especially as vendors promote the features that distinguish their solution from the others. Unlike much of SDN, the control plane protocols used in SD-WAN tend to be proprietary. But it is certainly true that SD-WAN did enough to reduce the complexity of building and managing encrypted tunnels to drive adoption of this approach, often replacing MPLS-based VPNs.

An important benefit offered by SD-WAN over many earlier VPN approaches was to simplify the task of managing access from a branch office to a cloud service offered by a third party. It seems natural that you would choose to access those services directly from an Internet-connected branch, but traditional VPNs would *backhaul* traffic to a central site before sending it out to the Internet, precisely so that security policies could be controlled centrally. With SD-WAN, the central control over security policy is achieved, while the data plane remains fully distributed–meaning that remote sites can directly connect to the cloud services without backhaul.

7.4.2 Mesh VPNs

Another approach to VPNs that combines some of the features of remote access VPNs and site-to-site VPNs is referred to as Mesh VPNs. Like a remote VPN, a mesh VPN builds tunnels that terminate directly on client devices. However, rather than connecting the other end of the tunnel to a central VPN gateway or concentrator, mesh VPNs build a mesh of tunnels among client devices. The effect is to create a VPN that interconnects the set of authorized client devices almost as if they were on the same private LAN, even though they can be located anywhere in the Internet.

There are numerous implementations of the mesh VPN approach, with Tailscale being a well-known implementation that contains a mixture of open source and proprietary components. Tailscale is built using WireGuard as the tunneling protocol, and adds a control and management plane to ease the task of setting up and managing the mesh. For example, WireGuard makes the assumption that public keys have been set up at the tunnel endpoints before the tunnel is established; Tailscale supplies a central coordination service to generate and distribute those keys.

One notable aspect of Tailscale is that it assumes that client devices are likely to be sitting in networks that use private addresses and are connected to the Internet through a NAT (network address translation) device. This problem doesn't exist when building a tunnel to a VPN concentrator with a public IP address, or between a pair of edge routers, but it has to be solved if you want to build client-to-client tunnels. There are quite a few details to getting this to work, especially given that NAT devices don't all behave the same way, and there may be firewalls to traverse as well. An IETF standard called STUN (Session Traversal Utilities for NAT) plays an important part, and the centralized control plane helps to resolve some of the more difficult corner cases. You can read more about the issues to be solved in Avery Pennarun's blog post.

Because mesh VPNs build tunnels all the way from client to client, they also avoid one of the drawbacks of traditional VPNs, which is the existence of trusted network zones, such as the network behind the firewall to which a remote access or site-to-site VPN would give access. In this respect they embrace the idea of zero trust networking, a topic we discuss in chapter 9.

Further Reading:

A. Pennarun. How Tailscale Works. Tailscale blog, 2020.

7.5 Web Authentication and Passkeys

While public key cryptography has been well understood for decades, and forms the basis for authentication of web sites using Transport Layer Security, its adoption for authentication of end-users has generally proven challenging. PGP was an early effort to allow end-users to authenticate themselves with public key cryptography, but its deployment remains limited. If you need to authenticate yourself to, say, your bank, it's overwhelmingly the case today that you will use some combination of user name (maybe an account number or an email address) and a password. Perhaps another factor, such as a one-time code generated locally by an app (referred to as a timed one-time password or TOTP) or a code sent over the cellular network to your phone, will also be used. Encryption (using TLS) prevents your password (and one-time code) from being seen by eavesdroppers when it is sent to the bank's site, but there are plenty of weaknesses to this form of authentication as we discuss below. Public key cryptography would generally be a better solution for the authentication of users but its deployment has been sparse historically. SSH, as noted in a previous section, supports the use of public keys for user authentication, but it's hardly in mainstream use by consumers on the Internet.

Password-based authentication had proven enormously problematic, with passwords frequently being compromised by a variety of attacks. If a user's password is obtained by an attacker, the attacker can now impersonate the user to authenticate himself. Passwords might be obtained using brute-force search, which works well on passwords that are relatively short or simple, and has become easier over time with increased computing power. Because many people reuse passwords across multiple sites, if a password is obtained from a breach of one site, it can often be used on other sites. And a range of *phishing attacks* entail somehow tricking a user into putting his login credentials into a fraudulent web site or divulging them over the phone. Phishing attacks are often initiated with an email leading the user to input his credentials to a domain name similar to the expected one, on a site that mimics the visual style of the legitimate web site. Multi-factor authentication raises the bar somewhat for the attacker, but even one-time codes can often be obtained via phishing attacks.

A range of efforts have been under way for many years to reduce the reliance on passwords and to drive adoption of public key cryptography for end-user authentication. The most visible recent development has been the appearance of *passkeys*, which, as the name suggests, are a form of user authentication that replaces passwords with public key-based authentication. The challenge is to automate key management on behalf of the user.

Passkeys are formally known as *discoverable credentials* and are defined in the Web Authentication (WebAuthn) specification of the W3C (World Wide Web Consortium). This work evolved from several prior efforts including those of the FIDO alliance (FIDO = Fast Identity Online).

The basic idea behind passkeys is simple: a user (or more likely, a device owned by the user) creates a private/public key pair specifically for a single web site and provides the public key to the site. The user proves their identity to the web site using some other method such as a previously established user name and password. The web site stores the public key for subsequent use. The next time that the user wants to authenticate to the web site, the site issues a challenge to the user, who uses the locally stored private key to sign their response to the challenge. The web site uses the stored public key to authenticate the user. Said another way, if you are familiar with SSH's use of public/private key pairs to authenticate a user logging into a remote server, you understand how passkeys are used to log into a remote web service.

The fact that the process is bootstrapped by getting the user to authenticate using a traditional approach (such as user name and password) is clearly a bit of a weakness. At the same time, it solves the thorny problem of how to scalably bind public keys to users which has proven challenging to date. Additional steps to secure the initial authentication might include the use of multi-factor authentication.

Passkeys offer two protections against phishing. First, the private key is never transmitted, being used only to sign the response to a challenge. Second, passkeys are bound to a specific web site. So a user will have a different private/public key pair for every web site they want to authenticate to. When the authentication challenge is received from the web site, the client-side software checks that it is coming from the correct web site using the standard authentication methods of TLS. A fraudulent web site will fail this check, so the user will not try to authenticate to the site.

Of course, if passkeys are to be effective as a phishing-prevention tool, they need to *replace* passwords, not just supplement them. If passwords remain available as an alternative, it seems safe to assume that attackers will keep using that option to breach user accounts. This is one of the problems that needs to be addressed in the deployment of passkeys.

The WebAuthn spec allows for considerable implementation flexibility, but there are two broad categories of passkey implementation. One approach binds the key to a specific piece of hardware, such as a USB key. Such keys have been around for many years and known by various names as the commercial offerings and standards around them have evolved. The generic names include U2F (universal second factor) and FIDO (from the FIDO Alliance).

Now that biometric authentication, such as facial and fingerprint recognition, is available on many devices, it is common to require biometric authentication to access a passkey. So a passkey might be stored on a mobile phone and require facial recognition of the owner before the passkey can be accessed.

The second class of passkey implementation allows the credentials to be copied among multiple devices, typically using some sort of password manager to keep the credentials secure and synchronized across devices. In this case, the private/public key pair is stored in the password manager and then is made available to the user across different devices (laptops, mobile phones, etc.) when they need the passkey.

There are strengths and weaknesses for each approach. Hardware tokens make phishing attacks almost impossible, since the only way to get access to the user's credential is to have physical access to the key. A password manager, on the other hand, is a piece of software that normally has some cloud service behind it to handle synchronization across devices. If an attacker manages to get access to the credentials necessary to log in to the cloud service, then they have access to the passkeys stored within it. For this reason (among others) password managers are generally secured with some sort of multi-factor authentication. One of those factors might be biometric, or even a hardware token.

The downside of hardware tokens is that the private key is stored only in one place. If the hardware token is lost, there is no way to recover the private key, so some other authentication method is needed as a backup. Also, since most hardware tokens lack biometric authentication, it is possible that a private key could be obtained and used by an attacker if he can gain access to the physical key.

Many of the important details of WebAuthn come down to making public key cryptography accessible to average users, rather than just the domain of the tech-savvy. This is where PGP, for example, has struggled to gain wider acceptance. WebAuthn is now part of the standards that are widely implemented for the World Wide Web, meaning that there are implementations across many browsers and web servers. There is also a well-defined API to allow authentication devices (such as FIDO keys) to communicate with browsers to manage the creation and use of private/public key pairs.

We are still in the relatively early days of passkeys as they start to become available on a wide variety of operating systems and web sites. Those who have led their development hope that they start to replace the ubiquitous password for user authentication.

7.6 Wireless Security

Wireless links are particularly exposed to security threats due to the lack of any physical security on the medium. While the convenience of 802.11 (Wi-Fi) and the Mobile Cellular Network (5G) has prompted widespread acceptance of the technology, concerns about security have been a recurring topic. This section looks at how the two dominant wireless technologies address the issue.

Note that securing a wireless link can be viewed as an example of defense in depth introduced in Chapter 2. As long as your transport layer connection is secured by TLS and/or your VPN securely tunnels over the public Internet using IPsec, the confidentiality of your communication is ensured; securing the wireless link is partially redundant. Not all users are that careful, of course, but there are also control packets exchanged between the wireless device and the wired infrastructure, and that communication must be secured.

7.6.1 Wi-Fi

It has long been understood how easy it is for an employee of a corporation to connect an 802.11 access point to the corporate network. Since radio waves pass through most walls, if the access point lacks the correct security measures, an attacker can now gain access to the corporate network from outside the building. Similarly, a computer with a wireless network adaptor inside the building could connect to an access point outside the building, potentially exposing it to attack, not to mention the rest of the corporate network if that same computer has, say, an Ethernet connection as well.

Consequently, there has been considerable work on securing Wi-Fi links. The IEEE 802.11i standard provides authentication, message integrity, and confidentiality to 802.11 (Wi-Fi) at the link layer. *WPA3*

(Wi-Fi Protected Access 3) is often used as a synonym for 802.11i, although it is technically a trademark of the Wi-Fi Alliance that certifies product compliance with 802.11i.

For backward compatibility, 802.11i includes definitions of first-generation security algorithms—including Wired Equivalent Privacy (WEP)—that are now known to have major security flaws. We will focus here on 802.11i's newer, stronger algorithms.

802.11i authentication supports two modes. In either mode, the end result of successful authentication is a shared Pairwise Master Key. *Personal mode*, also known as *Pre-Shared Key (PSK) mode*, provides weaker security but is more convenient and economical for situations like a home 802.11 network. The wireless device and the Access Point (AP) are preconfigured with a shared *passphrase*—essentially a very long password—from which the Pairwise Master Key is cryptographically derived.

802.11i's stronger authentication mode is based on the IEEE 802.1X framework for controlling access to a LAN, which uses an Authentication Server (AS) as in Figure 21. The AS and AP must be connected by a secure channel and could even be implemented as a single box, but they are logically separate. The AP forwards authentication messages between the wireless device and the AS. The protocol used for authentication is called the *Extensible Authentication Protocol* (EAP). EAP is designed to support multiple authentication methods—smart cards, Kerberos, one-time passwords, public key authentication, and so on—as well as both one-sided and mutual authentication. So EAP is better thought of as an authentication framework than a protocol. Specific EAP-compliant protocols, of which there are many, are called *EAP methods*. For example, EAP-TLS is an EAP method based on TLS authentication.

802.11i does not place any restrictions on what the EAP method can use as a basis for authentication. It does, however, require an EAP method that performs *mutual* authentication, because not only do we want to prevent an adversary from accessing the network via our AP, we also want to prevent an adversary from fooling our wireless devices with a bogus, malicious AP. The end result of a successful authentication is a Pairwise Master Key shared between the wireless

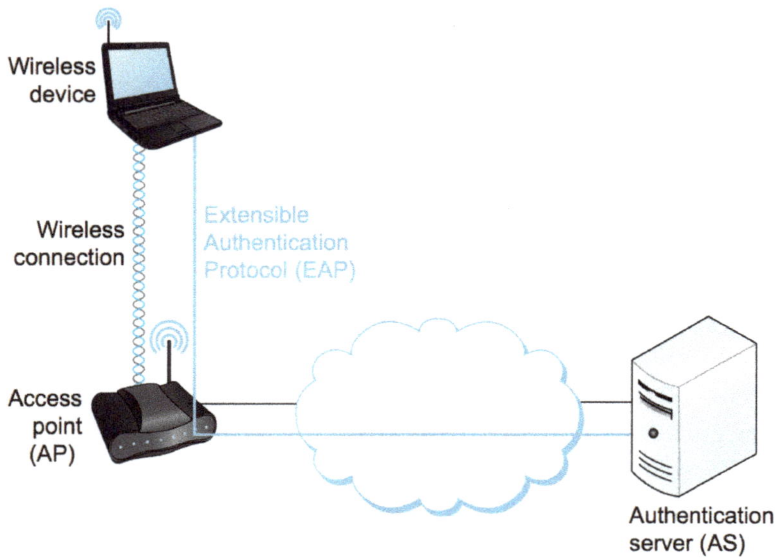

Figure 21: Use of an Authentication Server in 802.11i.

device and the AS, which the AS then conveys to the AP.

One of the main differences between the stronger AS-based mode and the weaker personal mode is that the former readily supports a unique key per client. This in turn makes it easier to change the set of clients that can authenticate themselves (e.g., to revoke access to one client) without needing to change the secret stored in every client.

With a Pairwise Master Key in hand, the wireless device and the AP execute a session key establishment protocol called the 4-way handshake to establish a Pairwise Transient Key. This Pairwise Transient Key is really a collection of keys that includes a session key called a *Temporal Key*. This session key is used by the protocol, called *CCMP*, that provides 802.11i's data confidentiality and integrity.

CCMP stands for CTR (Counter Mode) with CBC-MAC (Cipher-Block Chaining with Message Authentication Code) Protocol. CCMP uses AES in counter mode to encrypt for confidentiality. Recall that in counter mode encryption successive values of a counter are incorporated into the encryption of successive blocks of plaintext.

CCMP uses a Message Authentication Code (MAC) as an authenticator. The MAC algorithm is based on CBC, even though CCMP doesn't use CBC in the confidentiality encryption. In effect, CBC is performed without transmitting any of the CBC-encrypted blocks, solely so that the last CBC-encrypted block can be used as a MAC (only its first 8 bytes are actually used). The role of initialization vector is played by a specially constructed first block that includes a 48-bit packet number—a sequence number. (The packet number is also incorporated in the confidentiality encryption and serves to expose replay attacks.) The MAC is subsequently encrypted along with the plaintext in order to prevent birthday attacks, which depend on finding different messages with the same authenticator.

7.6.2 Mobile Cellular Network

The other widely used wireless networking technology is the Mobile Cellular Network, today ubiquitously known as 5G. The biggest difference between 5G and Wi-Fi is that the Mobile Network Operator (MNO)—the counterpart of an enterprise network administrator—has more direct control over the devices that are allowed to connect to their network. Specifically, the MNO provides a Subscriber Identity Module (SIM) that must be present in the mobile device. This SIM contains a small database that includes (among several dozen parameters used to control the device) two values that play a central role in link security: (1) a unique *International Mobile Subscriber Identifier (IMSI)* and (2) a secret key.

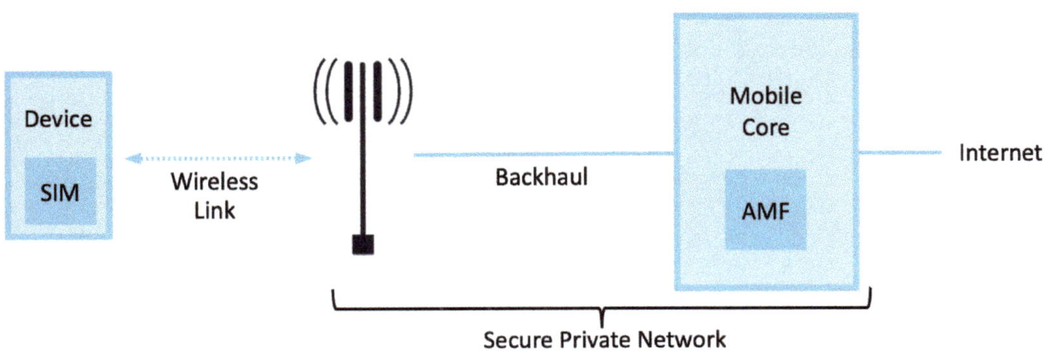

Figure 22: Device authentication in the Mobile Cellular Network.

When a device first becomes active, it communicates with a nearby base station over an unauthenticated radio channel. The base station, which is part of the *Radio Access Network (RAN)*, forwards the request to a backend system, known as the *Mobile Core*, over a secure backhaul connection. The Mobile Core is essentially an IP router that connects the RAN to the rest of the Internet, and among its many sub-components, an *Access and Mobility Management Function (AMF)* plays a central role in securing the wireless link on behalf of the newly connected device. Loosely speaking, the AMF is analogous to the AS used by Wi-Fi. For a more precise description of the Mobile Cellular Network, we recommend a companion book.

Further Reading:

L. Peterson, O. Sunay, and B. Davie. Private 5G: A Systems Approach..

Assuming the AMF recognizes the IMSI, it initiates an authentication protocol with the device. There are a set of options for authentication and encryption, but AES is commonly used. Note that this authentication exchange is initially in the clear since the base station to device channel is not yet secure.

Once the device and AMF are satisfied with each other's identity, the AMF informs the other sub-components of the Mobile Core and RAN of the parameters they will need to service the device (e.g., the IP address assigned to the device and the appropriate QoS parameters). It also instructs the base station to establish an encrypted channel to the device and sends the device the symmetric key it will subsequently use for the encrypted data channel with the base station. This symmetric key is encrypted using the public key of the device, so only the device can decrypt it. It does this using the secret key on its SIM card. Once complete, the device can use this encrypted channel to send and receive data over the wireless link to the base station.

Chapter 8. Infrastructure Security

In the preceding chapters we have focused on the security of end-systems connected to the Internet and on securing communication between parties as their traffic traverses the Internet. But the Internet itself consists of infrastructure, such as routers, that must also be defended against attacks. Two areas of particular concern are the interdomain routing system and the domain name system (DNS). Both systems routinely come under attack. They are also complex distributed systems. While distributing the routing and naming functions helps make these systems resilient to failure, many opportunities for attack exist. In this chapter we discuss some of the ongoing efforts to improve their resistance to attacks.[4]

[4] Many thanks to Cecilia Testart for her contributions to this chapter, particularly the BGP and Routing Security sections.

The following discussion builds on some of the concepts introduced in previous chapters. Notably, the concept of public key infrastructure (PKI), which we introduced in Chapter 4 and which underpins the operation of TLS, plays an important role in securing infrastructure as well. While the principles of certificates and chains of trust apply in any PKI, the specifics of how certificates are distributed and what they refer to are different in each application. We describe the different approaches to PKI for infrastructure services in the following sections.

Availability of infrastructure, including resistance to denial-of-service (DoS) attacks, is clearly important to the operation of the Internet. Mitigation of such attacks is increasingly handled by distributed infrastructure like content distribution networks (CDNs), as we discuss in the final section of this chapter.

8.1 BGP and Routing Security

In most respects, a router is just a special-purpose computer with some high-speed interfaces and specialized software to perform tasks such as route computation and advertisement. So routers need to be protected like end-systems, e.g., with strong passwords and multi-factor authentication, using access control lists and firewalls, etc. That is only a starting point, however, because the actual routing protocols themselves introduce opportunities for attack. BGP, the Border Gateway Protocol, is vulnerable to a wide range of attacks, and is the only routing protocol that is expected to cross the boundaries of a single administrative domain, so we focus our attention here.

The primary challenge in securing the Internet's routing infrastructure boils down to this: how can you trust a routing announcement received via BGP? At first glance, this looks similar to the problem solved by TLS: how do we know that we're talking to the web site we wanted to connect to? But there are multiple levels to this problem when it comes to inter-domain routing. When you have a secure, encrypted connection to your bank, you probably trust them to show you accurate information about your account (mostly—banks do make mistakes on occasions) and the secure connection protects it from modification by an attacker. A secure, encrypted connection to the website of the New York Times, however, doesn't mean you should believe every word published by the New York Times. Similarly, a secure connection to a BGP speaker (a router running BGP) doesn't imply that every route advertisement provided by that speaker is reliable. We need to look a bit more closely at how BGP works to see where the challenges lie.

BGP speakers advertise *paths* to reach *prefixes*. When a BGP speaker receives a set of path advertisements from its peers, it runs a route selection process to determine its preferred path to any prefix, using a large and flexible set of criteria to decide which path to select. The business relationships among providers play a central role in path selection. While a router might prefer a path to a given prefix that is shorter (as measured by the number of autonomous systems it contains) to one that is longer, that is not a hard rule (unlike intradomain routing). The business relationships among the different service providers and customers play a central role in the ultimate choice of path. When a BGP speaker has chosen a path to reach a particular prefix, it may choose to re-advertise that path to other BGP speakers, either in the same AS or in another AS. Again, this depends on customer-provider relationships. For a more full discussion of how BGP works, refer to the section on inter-domain routing in our main textbook.

A BGP speaker needs to trust that the paths that it is receiving from its peers are correct, and this turns out to be a multi-faceted challenge. Geoff Huston, the Chief Scientist at APNIC, has written a useful taxonomy of the threats that BGP faces, all of which relate to the trust among peers.

The taxonomy asks the following questions of the communication between two BGP speakers:

- How is the BGP session protected from modification or disruption?
- How does a speaker verify the identity of its peer?
- How does a speaker verify the authenticity and completeness of the routing information received from a peer?
- How does a speaker know that the advertisements received actually represent the true forwarding state of the peer?
- How current is the information received, and is it still valid?

The first two bullets are versions of the authentication and integrity issues that we addressed in Chapter 5. There are some details specific to BGP that we cover below. The remaining challenges all relate to the correctness of routing information carried by BGP and turn out to be more difficult to address.

Further Reading:

S. Murphy. BGP Security Vulnerabilitiess Analysis. RFC 4272, January 2006.

G. Huston. A Survey on Securing Inter-Domain Routing Part 1. BGP: Design, Threats and Security Requirements. APNIC Blog, August 2021.

L. Peterson and B. Davie. Computer Networks: A Systems Approach. Interdomain Routing.

8.1.1 Authentication and Integrity

Since BGP runs over a TCP connection, it was recommended for many years that the TCP connection be authenticated and integrity-protected using MD5 authentication. The MD5 authentication option for TCP is now viewed as insufficiently secure (due to known attacks on the MD5 algorithm). It also lacks dynamic key management and the ability to update the cryptographic algorithm, so it is now deprecated in favor of a more general TCP authentication option which is described in RFC 5925.

It might seem somewhat counterintuitive that BGP does not currently run over TLS, given the maturity and widespread adoption of that technology today. The explanation for this comes down to a combination of factors including history, inertia, and the different operational model of running BGP versus connecting to a remote website. For example, BGP sessions often run between directly connected routers at a peering point or Internet exchange points (IXPs) which allows for a simple TTL-based method to prevent spoofing. Privacy of BGP updates is considerably less important than authenticity. And as we shall see, there is a lot more to establishing the authenticity of a BGP advertisement that just authenticating the messages from a peer.

When BGP was being developed in the 1980s and 1990s, TLS was still far in the future, and packet encryption and decryption operations were generally quite computationally expensive. So it made sense that the initial focus was on authenticating messages, first using MD5 and then with updated algorithms, rather than providing the greater protection of encryption that TLS offers.

With this background, the idea of running BGP over TLS is an area of current research, and would offer potential benefits beyond simply adding privacy to BGP advertisements. Most notably, certificate management for TLS is now highly automated, which contrasts with the manual provisioning that must be performed when using MD5 or TCP-based authentication for BGP. The paper below on secure transport for BGP outlines this approach and suggests further enhancements that might further improve the security of BGP. However, in terms of the current state of the Internet, the recommended best practice for BGP sessions (described in RFC 7454) does not extend to running BGP over TLS.

Whether TLS or a more basic authentication mechanism is used, the effect is only to verify that the information came from the intended peer and has not been modified in transit. The much more challenging part of Internet routing security is in the validation of the routing information itself. When a peer announces a path to a certain prefix, how do we know that they really have this path?

8.1.2 *Correctness of Routing Information*

When a BGP speaker announces a path to a particular prefix, how do we know that they really have such a path? Do we know that they will use the path if asked to do so? Are they even authorized to use the path? The short answer to all these questions is that we don't know, but there has been a multi-decade quest to build mechanisms that enable greater confidence in the correctness of such announcements. This quest, and the slowness of its progress, was well documented by Sharon Goldberg in 2014. While progress continues today, a more recent study by Testart and Clark from 2021 indicated that progress had remained slow. There are a number of reasons for the lack of progress, as we discuss below.

Let's start with a simple and well-studied example. In 2008, ISPs in Pakistan were ordered by the government to block access to YouTube for users in the country. One ISP (Pakistan Telecom) chose to do this by advertising a route to a prefix that was within the range allocated to YouTube. In effect, the ISP announced "I have a good path to YouTube" so that it could then redirect traffic that would try to follow that path. The problem was that not only was this path not a viable way to reach YouTube, it was also a *more specific* path, that is, it was for a longer prefix than the true path to YouTube that was being advertised by other ASes. Since IP forwarding is based on the longest matching prefix in the routing table ("longest-prefix match") the more specific path overrides the less specific path when packets match the longer prefix. This turned into a problem well beyond the boundaries of Pakistan when the ISP advertised the route upstream to a larger ISP. The upstream ISP now saw the more specific route as a distinct piece of routing information from the true, less specific route, and so it re-advertised this (false) path to its peers. Repeated application of this decision to accept the more specific path and re-advertise it caused much of the Internet to view the small ISP in Pakistan as a true

Further Reading:

T. Wirtgen, N. Rybowski, C. Pelsser, O. Bonaventure. The Multiple Benefits of Secure Transport for BGP. ACM CONEXT, December 2024.

J. Durand, I. Pepelnjak and G. Doering. BGP Operations and Security. RFC 7454, February 2015.

path to YouTube. Within minutes a large percentage of the Internet was sending YouTube request traffic to Pakistan, causing a global outage for YouTube. Resolution was achieved by manual intervention at multiple ISPs to stop the global advertisement of the false path.

There are many other forms of attack possible on BGP, but they mostly take the form of a route being advertised and then propagated when it should not be. There is a relatively simple measure that should have prevented the incident described above: the provider AS immediately upstream from Pakistan Telecom should not have accepted the advertisement that said "I have a route to YouTube". How would it know not to accept this? After all, BGP needs to be dynamic, so a newly advertised prefix is often going to be correct. One solution to this problem is the use of Internet Routing Registries (IRRs), which serve as databases mapping address prefixes to the ASes that are authorized to advertise them. In the prior example, since YouTube is not a customer of Pakistan Telecom, the IRR would show that the YouTube prefix should not be advertised by this AS. The responsibility to filter out the false announcement falls on the *upstream* ISP, who would need to periodically query one or more IRRs in order to maintain an up-to-date set of filters to apply to its downstream peers.

There are numerous issues with the IRR approach, including that this sort of filtering gets much more difficult the closer you get to the "core" of the Internet. It's one thing to filter prefixes from an ISP that serves a modest number of customers in a single country; it's another to filter prefixes coming from a large peer with global presence. Some obviously bad routes can be filtered but it's very hard to get a complete picture sufficient to rule out anything incorrect that could be advertised. The set of rules that need to be configured on a BGP router for an ISP that carries hundreds of thousands of routes can also get very large.

There is also a question of whether all the information provided by an IRR can be trusted. We discuss approaches to building trust in the information provided by an IRR below.

Furthermore, as noted by in the article "*Why Is It Taking So Long to Secure Internet Routing?*", the incentives for prefix filtering are not well aligned. The cost of filtering falls on the AS that is immediately upstream of the misbehaving ISP, while the benefit accrues to some distant entity (YouTube in our example) who avoids the impact to their traffic thanks to the work of a provider with whom they have no relationship.

A more sophisticated approach relies on the use of cryptographically signed statements authorizing a particular AS to advertise paths to a particular prefix. This technology behind this is referred to as RPKI: Resource Public Key Infrastructure. RPKI builds on the concepts of cryptographic signatures and certificate hierarchies that we introduced in previous chapters.

RPKI provides a means by which entities involved in routing, such as the operator of an AS, can make assertions about information that is related to the advertisement of routes. These assertions take various forms depending on which part of the problem they aim to solve. We describe three different uses of the RPKI in the following sections.

Further Reading:

S. Goldberg. Why Is It Taking So Long to Secure Internet Routing? ACM Queue, August 2014.

C. Testart and D. Clark. A Data-Driven Approach to Understanding the State of Internet Routing Security. TPRC 48, February 2021.

8.1.3 Route Origin Validation (ROV)

The first use of RPKI is to allow an AS to prove that it is authorized to originate routing advertisements for specific address prefixes. A Route Origin Authorization (ROA) contains a certificate, an AS number, and a set of prefixes that the AS is authorized to advertise. The ROA is cryptographically signed by an entity that is itself trusted to provide this authorization, generally the organization to which this address prefix has been allocated. For example, an ISP typically is allocated a certain set of prefixes and may originate routing advertisements for those prefixes. An ROA allows the ISP to assert that it has the authority to make such an announcement, and for BGP speakers elsewhere in the Internet to validate that assertion.

Address allocation in the Internet is a hierarchical process. Regional Internet Registries (RIRs) are at the top of the hierarchy for address allocation. Their position in the hierarchy of address allocation makes them a logical place for the RPKI roots of trust, known as trust anchors. There are five RIRs globally (ARIN, RIPE, APNIC, AFRINIC and LACNIC) and each has a root certificate in the RPKI.

Hierarchical address allocation operates in the following manner.

An RIR can allocate a chunk of address space to an ISP, and the ISP can sub-allocate from that chunk to each of its customers. There may be additional layers in this hierarchy. A hierarchy of certificates can be created to follow this hierarchy of address allocation. The RIRs form trust anchors from which chains of trust can be built, much the way a modern browser comes with a set of trusted root certificate authorities (CAs) so that the certificates issued by web sites, which are signed by CAs, can be checked for validity.

A key distinction between RPKI and the certificates that we are familiar with from TLS is this: the certificates in TLS are used to validate the *identity* of a web site (e.g., a certificate for cnn.com tells your browser that it is actually talking to the entity that operates cnn.com), whereas RPKI certificates are used to validate the *resources* allocated to an entity such as an ISP or an end customer. The resources in the case of ROA certificates are IP address prefixes. As IP address allocation starts with the RIRs and proceeds down through ISPs to end customers, resource certificates are generated at each level in the hierarchy.

Figure 23: Chain of trust for RPKI

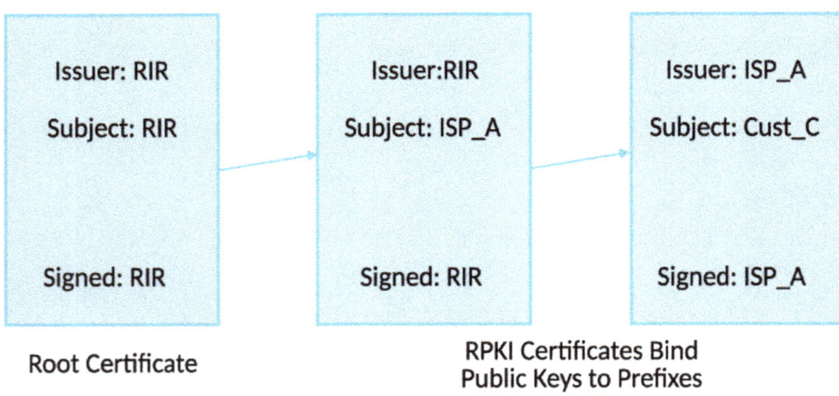

Figure 23 shows how the certificates are arranged for a simple example of an ISP *A* with customer *C*. There is a chain of trust from the root certificate to the customer, much like the sort of certification hierarchy we have seen used for TLS. However, because the goal here is ultimately to certify the authority of a certain AS to advertise a prefix, the details of the certificates are different from those used in TLS. For example, the certificate that ISP *A* issues, on the far right of the picture, says that some address prefix has been allocated to customer *C*, and includes the public key of customer C. This certificate is signed by ISP *A* using the private key of *A*. So if we can trust *A*, we learn two things about C: its public key and the set of addresses allocated to the holder of that public key. Note that we don't learn who *C* is (unlike a TLS certificate); we just learn the public key of the entity that is authorized to originate routing advertisements for some prefix or prefixes.

One level higher in the chain, the Regional Internet Registry (RIR) has issued a certificate that states ISP *A* has authority to allocate addresses out of some prefix. The prefix that *A* has allocated to C must be a subprefix within the allocation made by the RIR. By following the chain back to the root certificate, it is possible to establish that *C* is legitimately able to advertise the prefix allocated to it by *A*.

At this point we have created a set of bindings between public keys, which are held by entities such as Internet Registries, ISPs, and end customers, and IP address prefixes allocated to those entities. The next step is to create a Route Origin Authorization (ROA), which is a cryptographically signed object that associates a prefix with an AS that is authorized to originate routing advertisements for that prefix.

In our example above, C creates an ROA which it signs with its private key. The ROA contains the AS number of C and the prefix or prefixes that it wishes to advertise. Anyone who looks at the ROA and the resource certificate chain that leads from the root CA to C can validate that it has been signed with the private key belonging to C; they can also check that C is authorized to advertise the prefixes contained in the ROA. Because the ROA also contains the AS number for C, we now know that we should trust advertisements of this prefix if they originate from the stated AS. Furthermore, an ROA may limit the maximum length of the prefix to protect against bogus advertisements of more specific routes to a sub-prefix.

Rather than being passed around in real time like certificates in TLS, the RPKI certificates and ROAs are stored in repositories, which are typically operated by the RIRs. Address allocations happen at a

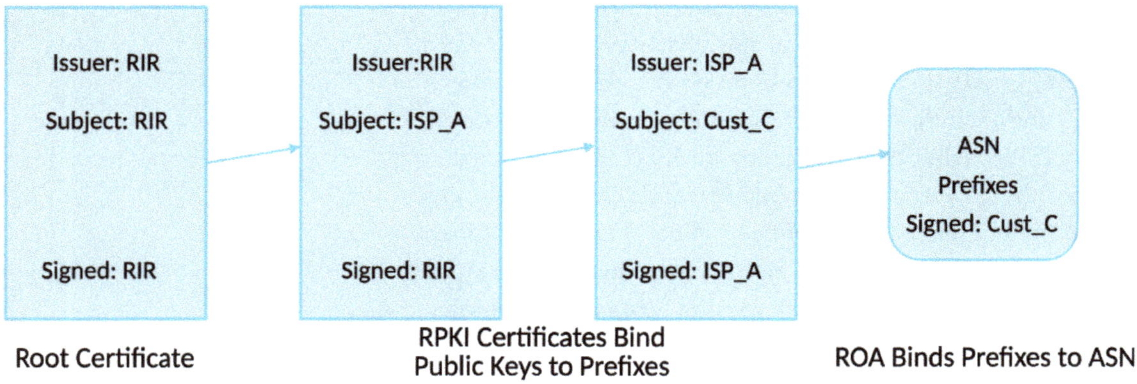

Figure 24: An ROA has a chain of trust back to the RPKI root

relatively long timescale, and certificates can be issued at the same time. Thus it is feasible to fetch the entire contents of the RPKI repository to build up a complete picture of the chains of certificates and signed ROAs that have been issued. With this information, ISPs use validation tools to determine *in advance* which ASes could originate routing advertisements for which prefixes. When a router that participates in BGP receives a new announcement, it can check its validity against the local validation tool.

Note the contrast to prior uses of certificates we have seen: a local validator builds a complete picture of the certificate hierarchy *a priori* in readiness for subsequent routing decisions, rather than checking the validity of certificates as part of establishing a session (as happens in TLS, for example). The repositories now become an essential part of our routing infrastructure and must themselves be secured and protected against DoS attacks.

There is a well-established set of software tools to automate the process of leveraging the RPKI for popular operating systems and commercial routing platforms. Notably, the routers running BGP do not perform cryptographic operations in real time when processing route advertisements; all the cryptographic operations happen in advance on servers that are external to the routers. The external validator systems answer queries about the validity of BGP advertisements based on information they download from the RPKI repository.

With the RPKI in place it is now possible to perform Route Origin Validation (ROV). That is, if a given AS claims to be the originator of a certain prefix, that claim can be checked against the information in the RPKI. So, for example, if Pakistan Telecom were now to claim to be the origin AS for a subprefix of YouTube, that could immediately be detected as false information and discarded by any router receiving such an advertisement, not just the neighbors of the offending ISP.

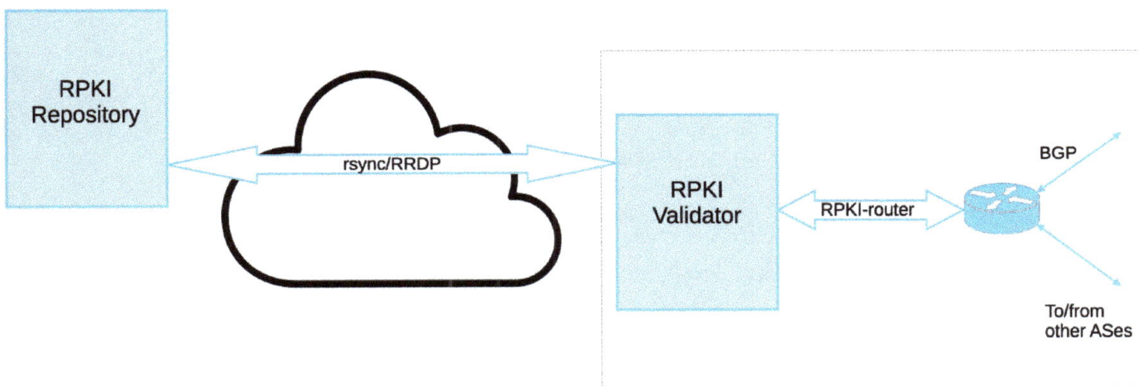

Figure 25: Each AS maintains a local cache of the RPKI repository, and BGP speakers query the local cache, allowing them to validate BGP advertisements.

Some of the practical aspects of ROV are shown in Figure 25. An AS performing route origin validation maintains a local cache of the RPKI repository, which is fetched using rsync or the RPKI Repository Delta Protocol (RRDP). A BGP speaker in the AS retrieves the set of valid ROAs by querying the local cache, using another protocol called the RPKI-to-router (RTR) protocol. This protocol allows the router to receive periodic updates to the set of valid ROAs from the local cache. Using this information, the router is able to check the validity of the originating AS in BGP advertisements that it receives from other ASes.

While there are many forms of attack or misconfiguration that would not be caught by ROV (particularly an AS falsely advertising a path that doesn't actually exist to a valid originating AS) it does prevent a large number of issues, especially those caused by misconfiguration. To more fully combat the advertisement of false information in BGP, it is necessary to adopt some sort of path validation, as discussed below.

The adoption of RPKI for route origin validation has been moving along steadily for several years now. The adoption of ROAs is tracked by NIST (the National Institute of Standards and Technology in the U.S.)—see the Further Reading section. At the time of writing, the NIST RPKI monitor indicates that of the one-million-plus routes advertised globally in BGP, about 56% are covered by valid ROAs. Less than 2% are detected as invalid (the ROV check fails) while the remaining 42% do not contain ROA information. Looking at the deployment over time we can see a steady increase in valid ROA and a corresponding decrease in the "not found" group—the advertisements with no ROA. While 56% is a long way from 100%, this level of penetration is a significant accomplishment—especially given the historical difficulty of making changes to Internet routing and the "core" of the Internet.

One final point of note about the RPKI is that, just like other forms of certificate infrastructure, it relies on Certificate Revocation Lists (CRLs) to revoke certificates. This is important for handling cases such as the re-allocation of an address prefix from one provider to another. The good news is that CRLs are distributed from the RPKI repositories just like other objects in the RPKI.

Further Reading:

NIST. RPKI Monitor (`https://rpki-monitor.antd.nist.gov/ROV`).

8.1.4 Path Validation (BGPsec)

Route origin validation only tackles part of the problem with BGP security. Even if the originating AS can be shown to be valid, what do we know about the rest of the path? For example, if a malicious ISP has a valid path to a certain prefix that traverses five ASes, but chooses to falsely advertise that it can reach that prefix in two AS hops, it is likely to attract traffic destined for that prefix. Whatever the motive for such a step may be (e.g., to increase revenue or to censor certain traffic, or even simple misconfiguration) it clearly undermines the correct operation of Internet routing. The solution to such attacks is to validate not just the originator of a prefix but the entire path. It turns out this is a considerably harder problem to solve than ROV.

There are a few different proposals for how to securely validate paths. We focus here on the BGPsec standard from the IETF which illustrates the overall approach and the challenges with achieving widespread deployment.

In contrast to ROV, BGPsec path validation relies on cryptographic operations being adopted as part of BGP itself. Each BGP speaker (router) taking part in path validation signs its BGP announcements using a private key specific to the router. The public key corresponding to such a private key is included in a certificate that is published in the RPKI. Such certificates also include the AS number or numbers corresponding to the AS in which the router is located.

As with all public key certificates, we need a chain of trust from a trusted root to the router certificate. For example, an RIR could provide the root of trust, and sign certificates for ISPs, who could then act as the certificate authorities for their own routers. The use of the word "could" in this paragraph reflects the lack of real-world deployment of BGPsec.

With a certificate hierarchy in place, anyone receiving such a BGP announcement can verify that it came from a router within the AS that it claims to represent, and that it has not been modified in transit. The RPKI enables the recipient to obtain the public key corresponding to the announcing AS and thus validate the message.

The harder part of the problem is validating that the *contents* of the message are correct from the perspective of BGP. Since a BGP announcement is an ordered list of ASes, each of which has added itself into the path to the destination, we need to validate that every AS in the path has correctly announced a route to the destination when it added itself into the path.

The way this is achieved is to have every router that adds an AS to the path sign its announcement. We saw above that the RPKI could be used to create bindings between public keys and entities authorized to advertise a particular prefix. For path validation, we use the RPKI to create bindings between public keys and Autonomous Systems. With the RPKI in place, every router participating in BGPsec can be assumed to have a well-known public key and matching private key.

Now consider the process of constructing a path to a particular prefix. The path consists of a set of ASes. For example, a router in AS1, the origin AS, signs an announcement that says it is the origin for the prefix, using its private key. Furthermore, it includes the number of the target AS, AS2, to which it is sending the announcement, in the set of fields covered by the signature. Thus, we end up with a message that says "AS1 can reach prefix P and has sent this information to AS2" signed by a router from AS1.

A router in AS2 receives this announcement, and, having validated the signature, it can now add itself to the path. The router in AS2 can now issue a signed announcement that says "the path <AS2,AS1> leads to prefix P" and sign this using its private key. It includes the full signed message from AS1 as well as the new path. Again, before signing, it includes the number of the target AS to which it is sending this announcement. This announcement is received by AS3 which can now add itself to the path and sign the result, and so on.

Including the target AS in the material that is signed is essential to the correct operation of BGPsec. Suppose that, for example, AS3 tries to lie about the path it has to AS1, claiming that the path <AS3,AS1> is valid (skipping over AS2). It can't construct a valid message to make this claim with the information that it received from AS2, because AS2 is the target given by AS1. An attempt to create a signed path <AS3,AS1> could be detected as invalid, because the signed statement from AS1 indicates that its target was AS2, not AS3.

Thus, when a valid signed announcement is received, the receiver is able to validate that every AS in the chain to the destination has received an announcement of the rest of the path to the destination. While this still does not prove that the path to the destination will actually be able to carry data, it does prove that a set of announcements made their way along the stated path. It remains a possibility that some AS might have advertised a path that it will not honor—AS2, for example, might refuse (or be unable) to forward traffic from AS3 to AS1 in spite of having advertised the path. A particular concern is route leaks, in which misconfiguration causes an AS to advertise a route by mistake, with no intention of attracting traffic to that prefix. When such traffic arrives it might overwhelm the resources of the AS that accidentally advertised the route, causing traffic to be dropped.

Compared to ROV, the deployment story for path validation using BGPsec is disappointing. We've only described one of several proposals to cryptographically validate the paths advertised in BGP, but the sad fact is that there is little to no deployment of any of them. There are at least two challenges with path validation that contribute to this situation. One is that it is relatively costly to start performing cryptographic operations as part of BGP (in contrast to ROV, where cryptographic operations happen separately from the validation of BGP messages). The second is a "collective action problem": when a single ISP pays the cost of implementing BGPsec, it does little if anything to improve the situation for that ISP. Only when a critical mass of ISPs are using BGPsec does it start to provide significant incremental benefits over ROV. Issuing an ROA, by contrast, immediately helps the provider who issues it. The situation is captured in the paper "BGP Security in Partial Deployment". An approach that holds promise to address both these issues is described in the following section.

Further Reading:

R. Lychev, S. Goldberg and M. Schapira. BGP security in partial deployment: is the juice worth the squeeze? ACM SIGCOMM, August 2013.

8.1.5 AS Provider Authorization (ASPA)

At the time of writing, there is an effort underway at the IETF to standardize an approach to path validation known as ASPA (AS Provider Authorization). The idea is to use a new set of objects in the RPKI to capture the relationships among ASes, and then use that information to check the validity of BGP advertisements as they are received.

ASPA shares an attractive property with ROV: no cryptographic operations are added to BGP itself. Just as ROV builds a database (in the RPKI) of who is allowed to originate an advertisement, ASPA builds a database showing which ASes provide transit to other ASes. This, too, uses the RPKI, but with different types of certificates, known as ASPA records.

An important ingredient in ASPA is the insight that the relationships between ASes can be placed into a small set of categories. First, if there is no BGP connection between a pair of ASes, they have no relationship—and hence we should never see this pair of ASes next to each other in an advertised path. For any pair of ASes that do interconnect, the relationship can normally be classified as customer-to-provider, or peer-to-peer. A customer depends on a provider to deliver traffic to and from their AS, and that means that it is expected that the provider's AS number will appear in routing advertisements to reach the customer AS. Customer ASes, on the other hand, only deliver traffic to their provider ASes if it originates in the customer AS itself or comes from the customer's customers.

The relationship between customers and providers is normally captured visually as "valley-free" routing. Routing advertisements flow "up" from customers to providers, then (optionally) across between peers, then down from providers to customers, as depicted in Figure 26. In this figure, customer ASes are depicted below their provider AS, while the two ASes at the top have a peer-to-peer relationship. Valley-free routes have the property that they never start to go down (towards customers) and then head up again towards providers. The appearance of a valley is a strong indication of a route leak. A database that establishes the customer-to-provider relationships gives us the ability to detect such anomalies.

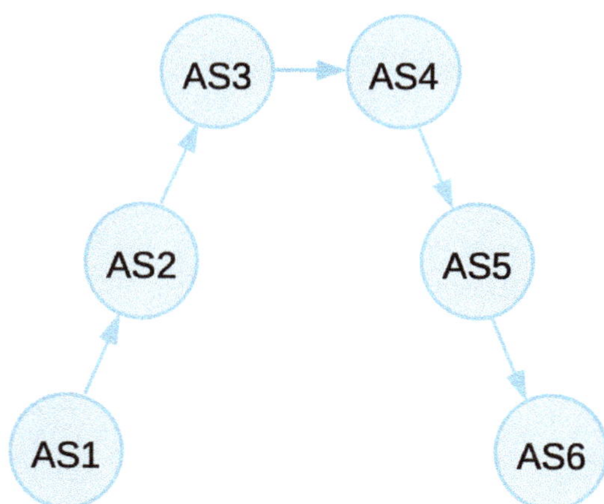

Figure 26: Valley-free topology of Autonomous Systems

Suppose that two ASes, X and Y, publish a list of their providers using ASPA objects in the RPKI. Let's say that there is an ASPA object from AS Y that asserts AS X is one of its providers, as well as an ASPA object from AS X that does not include AS Y among its providers. If a router receives an advertisement in which Y appears to be a provider for X, this is clearly wrong and the router drops the advertisement. The question of how we can tell that a particular AS is a provider, customer, or peer of another AS is a bit subtle, but it depends on the properties of valley-free routing. We can't have an arbitrary mix of customer-provider and provider-customer links in a valid path; there must be a set of paths going "up" towards providers followed by at most one lateral path followed by a set of paths going "down" towards customers. The more relationships that are placed in the RPKI, the more power a BGP speaker gains to detect paths that are invalid.

ASPA adds further security to the routing system beyond that offered by ROV, because it catches attacks where an AS announces routes where the origin AS is correct (i.e., covered by a valid ROA) but the path is not legitimate. Such attacks are known as forged-origin prefix hijacks.

Furthermore, ASPA catches some routing problems (such as accidental leakage of routes) that are not caught by BGPsec. This is because BGPsec shows that ASes are connected to each other but does not capture the customer-provider relationships. ASPA also provides benefits even if it is only partially deployed on a path, as the above example illustrates. In other words, it is amenable to incremental deployment.

Further Reading:

A. Azimov et al. BGP AS_PATH Verification Based on Autonomous System Provider Authorization (ASPA) Objects. Internet draft, work in progress.

8.2 DNS and Naming Security

The Domain Name System (DNS) is, like BGP, another critical component of the Internet's infrastructure that has come under repeated attack in the decades since it was first introduced. Also like BGP, it was developed in an era when attacks on the Internet were not a top concern of protocol designers.

If you need a refresher on how DNS operates, see the section in our main textbook listed below. DNS queries and responses are sent between name servers as UDP datagrams, unprotected by encryption or authentication. Thus, the recipient of a DNS response is unable to determine who sent it—just because it looks like a reply to the query doesn't mean it came from the server to which the query was sent. Nor can the recipient establish whether it contains valid information. And it turns out to be relatively easy to send false responses to DNS requests that can fool the recipients. Because of the way DNS caches responses, the impact of such false information can be widespread.

"Cache poisoning"—also sometimes referred to as DNS spoofing—is a common form of attack on DNS. If an attacker can either force a resolver to make a recursive query to an authoritative name server, or predict roughly when such a query is to be made, the attacker can try to send a fake response to *that* query. Figures 27 and 28 show an example.

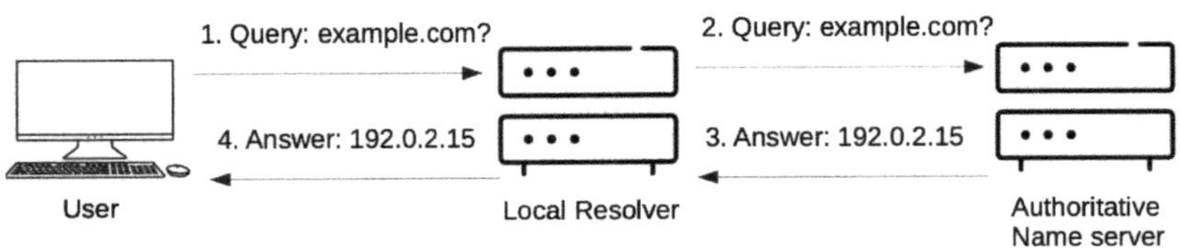

Figure 27: Example of DNS Resolution

When everything works as intended, a client machine makes a query to the local DNS resolver, which, finding nothing in its cache, sends a query to an authoritative name server. This is one of the simplest scenarios for name resolution when the answer is not already cached locally. (There will often be multiple queries required at step 2.) The answer is returned by the authoritative server and then cached and returned to the client. Subsequent requests for the same query from any client served by the local resolver can now be served from the resolver's cache without steps 2 and 3 taking place.

The cache poisoning attack depends on an attacker getting false information into the cache of a server, where it will stay until the TTL (time to live) for that information expires. A TTL is often on the order of an hour. There are many ways to do this; we sketch one possibility.

Suppose that the attacker is able to observe the client request (1) in Figure 27, perhaps by snooping on open WiFi. The attacker can now flood the resolver with fake versions of the expected response (3), hoping that with enough guesses they can generate a response that will be accepted by the resolver. The ID field in the DNS header is a

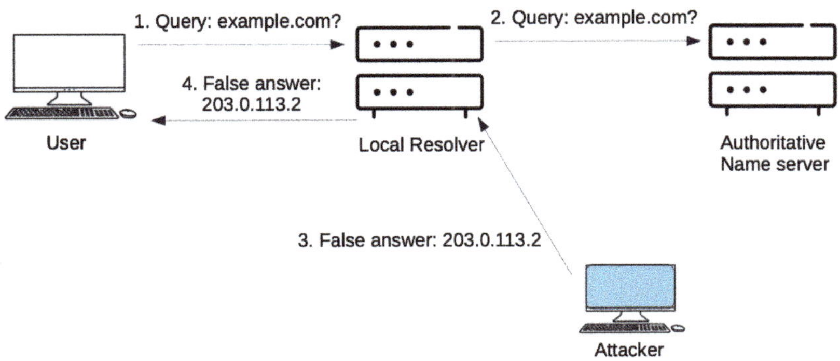

Figure 28: Attacker poisons DNS cache

16-bit field and the server UDP port associated with DNS is a well-known value, so there are only 2^{32} possible combinations of ID and client UDP port for a given client and server. That makes brute force attacks feasible.

Even with no visibility of the client traffic, the attacker can force the resolver to make queries to example.com by issuing queries of its own, and then send the flood of responses to impersonate the authoritative server. If successful, this leaves the fake data in the cache until its TTL expires. Other clients of the resolver will now get the bad result from the cache. There are many variations of this type of attack, broadly cataloged in RFC 3833, which analyzes the threats faced by DNS.

When the goal is to limit access to certain sites, rather than to redirect a client to a fake site, simply disrupting the process of DNS resolution is sufficient to make access to the target sites difficult for end users. The use of packet inspection to intercept DNS queries passing through a network and then to inject fake responses, or simply drop the query, is part of the suite of techniques used to control Internet access by national governments. See the Further Reading section for a thorough study on this phenomenon and its widespread effects in and beyond China.

Further Reading:

L. Peterson and B. Davie. Computer Networks: A Systems Approach. Name Service (DNS).

D. Atkins and R. Austein. Threat Analysis of the Domain Name System (DNS). RFC 3833, August 2004.

Anonymous. The Collateral Damage of Internet Censorship by DNS Injection. Computer Communications Review, July 2012.

8.2.1 DNS Amplification Attacks

There is a class of denial-of-service (DoS) attack that leverages the properties of DNS to attack other systems, rather than being an attack on DNS itself. Recall that DNS is UDP-based. A name server sends a response back to the IP address from which a query was sent, and since there is no TCP connection to establish, it is relatively easy to use a fake source address in a query. In this case, the name server can be tricked into sending traffic to some unsuspecting host. And it is not hard to see how this can be turned into a *distributed* denial-of-service attack: many hosts (e.g., a set of hosts in a botnet) can make coordinated requests to a set of name servers, with all the requests using the same spoofed source address. Not only does this lead to a lot of traffic heading to the target address, but the name servers can be make to perform a traffic *amplification* function, because the response to a DNS query can be much larger than the query that triggered it. In particular, the DNS query type "ANY" causes all records for a domain to be returned, which can be a lot of data returned for a simple query. The handling of such queries has recently been clarified in an RFC in a manner that should reduce the impact of ANY queries, but that is not a complete solution to DNS amplification attacks.

Three main steps can be taken to reduce these attacks. The first is to avoid the deployment of "open" resolvers, i.e., resolvers which will accept queries from anywhere. For example, the resolver for an enterprise should be configured such that only clients within that enterprise can send queries to it; it should not accept queries from the broader Internet.

The second step is source address validation. Source address filtering is a tool that can be applied at the boundaries of autonomous systems to reject traffic with spoofed source addresses. It may not be 100% effective but it will reduce the effectiveness of large scale attacks.

Finally, recall that there are general ways to deal with DoS attacks such as the use of content distribution networks and black-holing of DoS traffic. We discuss general approaches to DoS mitigation below.

8.2.2 DNS Security Extensions (DNSSEC)

Since DNS queries in the original design are unauthenticated, cleartext UDP datagrams, a natural approach to preventing attacks on DNS would be to use some of the techniques outlined in Chapter 5 to authenticate DNS responses. That is precisely what the first big effort to improve DNS security, the DNS Security Extensions (DNSSEC), does.

The first step for DNSSEC is similar to an approach we have seen used in other scenarios: to establish chains of trusted public keys using a hierarchy of certificates. Recall that in DNS we have an existing hierarchical relationship between zones, with the root zone at the top, so it is natural to establish a certificate hierarchy following the zone hierarchy. As a reminder, see the example hierarchy from the section on DNS in our main textbook, reproduced below.

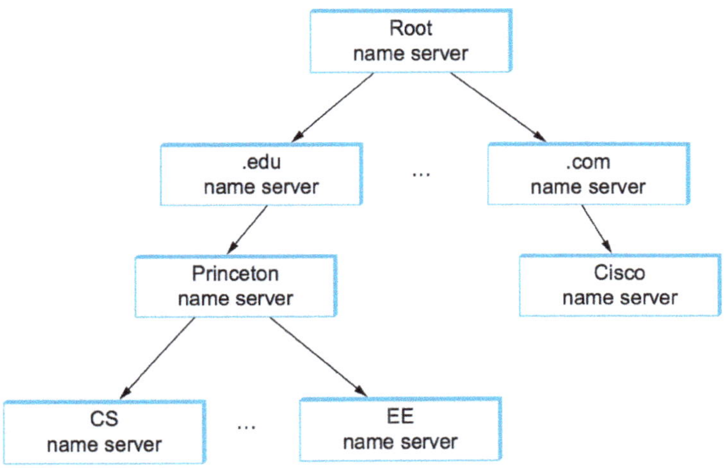

Figure 29: Hierarchy of DNS name servers

Suppose, for example, an administrator of the princeton.edu domain wants to start signing the responses issued by the nameserver they operate. They need to obtain a certificate for the public key that they plan to use, and that certificate will be issued and signed by the .edu domain. The .edu domain in turn requires a certificate to establish that their key can be trusted, and that certificate is issued and signed by the root domain. As with other systems such as TLS certificates, establishing a root of trust must be done by some out-of-band mechanism. There is actually an elaborate, formal process for generating the root key—a signing ceremony with multiple participants and auditors—that enables the keys for the root zone to be trusted.

While there are obvious similarities to the chains of trust used for TLS, the notable difference here is that the chain of certificates that must be followed is precisely defined by the hierarchy of the DNS. Whereas a TLS certificate could be issued by a range of certificate authorities, the certificates for any zone in DNSSEC must be issued by the parent zone. This has some advantages, such as limiting the opportunities for bad behavior by CAs that has occasionally occurred with TLS certificates. However, it also introduces a weakness: if your parent zone, or any zone in the path between the zone seeking a certificate and the root, is not using DNSSEC, then this zone is unable to use DNSSEC. To put it another way, DNSSEC starts at the top of the zone hierarchy and flows down to the leaves, and any zone along that path that fails to implement DNSSEC prevents its children from implementing DNSSEC. For example, using our figure above, if princeton.edu does not implement DNSSEC, the CS department would be out of luck if they wanted to implement it, since they could not get their key signed by the parent zone.

For a real-world example of DNSSEC in use, we set up the domain systemsapproach.org to use DNSSEC. To test that it was actually working, we used the open source tool DNSviz to check whether our zone was being correctly signed. DNSviz produces a detailed report that can be captured graphically, as shown in Figure 30. The main thing to observe in this figure is the 3-layer hierarchy from the root zone to the .org zone to the systemsapproach.org zone, where the parent zone signs the key for the child zone so that signatures from the child zone can then be validated by DNS resolvers.

The requirement to implement at every level from root to leaf is one of the barriers to DNSSEC adoption that is cited in an article by Geoff Huston of APNIC about the poor deployment of the technology (see Further Reading). Given that the work to secure DNS has been going on for over thirty years now, and it has yet to reach 40% deployment (based on measurements reported by APNIC and the Internet Society), it is reasonable to ask whether it is ever likely to succeed. Huston notes a number of other reasons why its success has been limited, not least of which is that TLS, while solving a different problem, somewhat sidesteps the need for validating DNS. If you know that you are connected to the correct web site using HTTPS because it has proven its identity using a TLS certificate that you trust, do you really care what IP address was used by the underlying protocols to connect you to the web site?

This is not to say that protecting DNS is unimportant, however. Interference with DNS is still a vector for censorship and surveillance of Internet usage. Subverting DNS to direct a client to a site other than the one they intended to reach undermines the operation of the Internet. While DNSSEC has struggled to gain traction, other methods of protecting DNS have appeared more recently and are having some impact, as discussed in the next section.

The challenges of securing DNS illustrate a point we made early in the book about the trusted computing base (TCB) and minimizing its size. If DNS needs to be trusted in order for systems that depend on the Internet to operate securely, then we have chosen a large, distributed system component that needs to be made secure. Having largely failed to make DNS secure over thirty years, it is a good thing that TLS (and other systems using end-to-end encryption) provides secure communications over untrusted infrastructure. In other words we have excluded DNS from the TCB.

A final note on DNSSEC is that, by making responses larger, it has the potential to worsen amplification attacks. The response to a request to a DNS server that implements DNSSEC contains both a signature and the key used to verify the signature. That's a significant increase in the number of bytes returned for a single query. The mitigation techniques outlined above—source address filtering and DoS prevention—can still be applied. Additionally, there is an advantage to using cryptographic algorithms that use relatively short keys. For this reason the ECDSA algorithm may be preferred to RSA, since ECDSA keys are considerably shorter than RSA keys for comparable levels of security.

This small detail illustrates how much of security consists of making tradeoffs. While adding DNSSEC is a positive in terms of securing the DNS itself, it has contributed to the risk of DoS attacks leveraging DNS amplification. Adding security almost always imposes some costs—it is important to be aware of them and to ensure that the payoff for an additional mechanism justifies its costs.

Further Reading:

G. Huston. Calling Time on DNSSEC? APNIC Blog, May 2024.

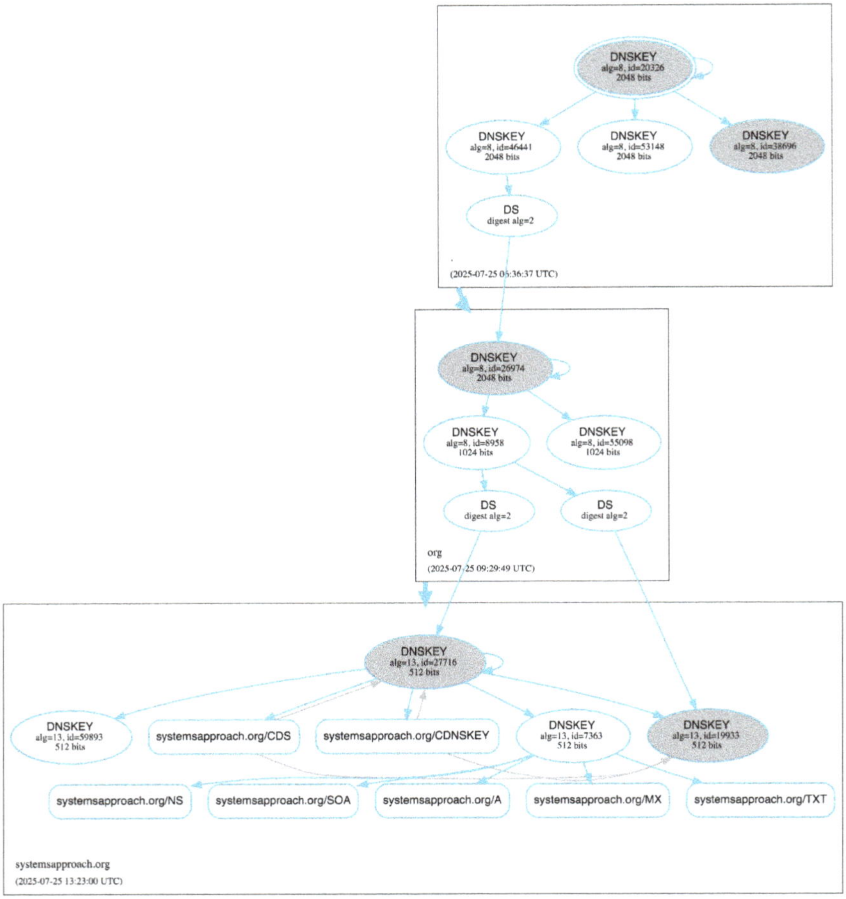

Figure 30: Validation of DNS keys and signatures by DNSviz

8.2.3 *Encrypted DNS (DoH, DoT, ODNS)*

With the widespread adoption of TLS to encrypt and authenticate HTTP traffic, as discussed in Chapter 6, it should come as no surprise that there are now standard ways to send DNS queries and responses over TLS-secured channels. There have been a few similar proposals to achieve this outcome, with the IETF having standardized both DNS over TLS (DoT) in RFC 7858, and DNS over HTTPS (DoH) in RFC 8484. There is some debate about the merits of each but for the purposes of our discussion the differences are not terribly significant.

The basic idea behind both approaches is simple enough. Rather than sending DNS queries and responses as plaintext UDP datagrams, the DNS client establishes a TLS or HTTPS connection to the DNS resolver, and then issues queries as requests within that encrypted channel. The details of how to encode the requests and responses are spelled out in the RFCs and we need not dwell on them here.

It's worth noting that, in contrast to DNSSEC, DoH and DoT provide no assurance that the DNS information being provided by the resolver is correct. We can be sure of the identity of the resolver we are connected to, since that is provided by its TLS certificate. And we know that the query sent and response issued by the resolver have not been modified or observed by an intermediary, since they are both encrypted and authenticated. But if the resolver itself is giving bad information, perhaps because the information provided to it from upstream in the DNS hierarchy has been corrupted, the client will be none the wiser. So while the need to deploy DNSSEC all the way along the hierarchy is something of an impediment to deployment, it does provide a level of security that isn't provided by simply securing the client-to-resolver channel.

Another notable security risk that is not addressed by any of the approaches discussed to this point is the privacy of the client making the queries. The resolver has access to all the client requests in unencrypted form, which would seem to be a requirement for those requests to be served. However, there have been efforts to improve the privacy of client requests using a technique known as *Oblivious DNS*.

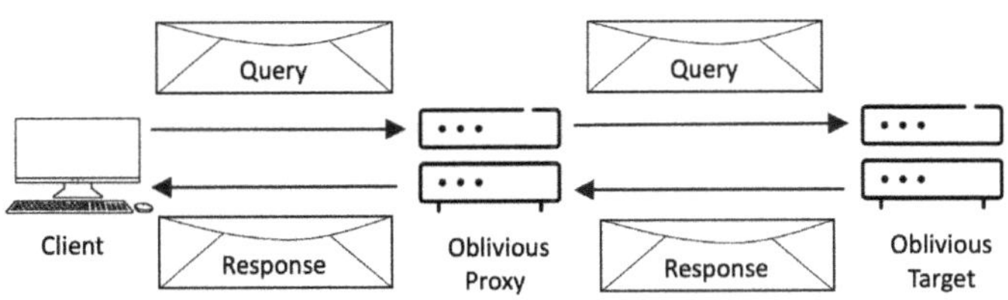

Figure 31: Oblivious DNS.

The central idea in oblivious DNS is to hide the identity of the client from the resolver. This is done by leveraging DoH to encrypt the requests from the client and the responses sent to the client, using a key that is associated with the target. But rather than send the queries direct to the target, as in standard DoH, oblivious DNS inserts a proxy between client and target. So the proxy gets an encrypted request that it cannot interpret, and then passes the request on to the target. The target can decrypt the request but doesn't know which client sent it, and sends an encrypted response back to the proxy. As long as the proxy supports a mix of clients, and and the proxy and target do not collude, neither of them has the information to figure out what queries a given client is making.

Oblivious DNS is an experimental protocol but there are some deployments already available of both the proxy and target behavior. Notably, Apple has built a privacy-focused service that combines oblivious DNS with several other technologies to support private browsing. Large CDN operators such as Cloudflare have support for the target function.

Further Reading:

Z. Hu, et al. Specification for DNS over Transport Layer Security (TLS). RFC 7858, May 2016.

P. Hoffman and P. McManus. DNS Queries over HTTPS (DoH). RFC 8484, October 2018.

P. Schmitt, A. Edmundson, A. Mankin, and N. Feamster. Oblivious DNS: Practical Privacy for DNS Queries. Proc. 2019 Applied Networking Research Workshop, 2019.

8.3 DoS Mitigation

In much of this book we have focused on attacks against the confidentiality or integrity of information, but we also need to concern ourselves with availability. This is true for both end systems (such as web sites) and the infrastructure of the network itself. Commonly known as *Denial of Service (DoS)* attacks, such attacks typically involve an adversary trying to overwhelm "good" resources (link bandwidth, packet forwarding rates, server response throughput) with traffic generated by "bad" resources (such as botnets constructed from a distributed collection of compromised devices). Patching of vulnerabilities and the deployment of security appliances such as firewalls can help protect devices from being compromised in the first place, but they are not perfect—new vulnerabilities appear constantly and a human is often the weakest link. Hence we also need ways to mitigate the impact of *Distributed DoS (DDoS)* attacks. This is another example of defense in depth: protect devices against being compromised, and also protect against the attacks launched by compromised devices.

Keeping in mind that DDoS traffic typically looks legitimate (there's just too much of it), the DDoS challenge is addressed by two general countermeasures. Note that the best we can hope for is to mitigate the impact of such attacks; there is no cure-all. This is easy to understand at an intuitive level: any systems that we deploy to defend against DoS attacks represent a kind of resource that can itself be DoSed. Thus DoS mitigation solutions tend to be distributed themselves.

The first countermeasure is to absorb potential attacks with even greater resources than the adversary is able to muster. For web content, this is done using the same mechanism as is used to absorb flash crowds of legitimate traffic: a *Content Distribution Network (CDN)*. The idea is to replicate content (whether it's a movie or a critical piece of infrastructure metadata) across many widely-distributed servers. As long as the aggregate capacity of these servers is greater than the aggregate capacity of the botnet—and the CDN does a good job spreading requests across the available servers—content remains available. This notion of *aggregate* capacity generalizes beyond web servers responding to HTTP GET requests. A network is itself a distributed collection of forwarding and transmission resources, engineered to distribute those resources in a way that avoids vulnerable bottlenecks. The DNS illustrates this perfectly: it is a highly distributed system designed to avoid single points of failure with redundancy at all levels of the hierarchy.

The second countermeasure is to filter malicious traffic as early (close to the source) as possible. If a DoS attack comes from a single source, then it is easy to "block" traffic from that source at an ingress to a network you control. This is why DoS attacks are typically distributed. Dropping (or rate limiting) attack packets at the boundary router for a service provider (or at a firewall for an enterprise) is better than allowing those packets to flood the core of the network and reach a victim server(s), but the more widely distributed the periphery of your network, the earlier you can filter malicious packets. And drawing on the first countermeasure, the more widely distributed your network resources are, the greater your aggregate filtering capacity. Global overlay networks, as provided by companies like Cloudflare and Fastly, offer a combination of content distribution and distributed packet filtering. These are commercial products, with many proprietary details, but the general principles outlined here explain their underlying strategy.

Finally, note that DoS attacks highlight the never-ending nature of tackling security. Almost any protocol or system can by a target of a DoS attack. We discussed the role of DNS in amplification of DoS attacks in the preceding section. When attacks are launched against web sites, attackers are often taking advantage of the HTTP protocol—significant server resources are consumed responding to bogus GET requests. As a very different example, the forwarding of IP packets can be attacked with a "Christmas Tree" packet, one that has multiple options turned on (i.e., is "lit up like a Christmas tree"), where each option requires IP to execute instructions it would not normally execute to forward a typical packet. A router with a naive implementation of IP would be at risk of not being able to forward packets at line speed if it's busy processing the options. For this reason, routers typically implement a "fast path" that is able to keep pace with line speeds and a "slow path" that processes exceptional packets, and most importantly, they quickly determine which path each packet should be assigned to. This is a variant of the second countermeasure—decide early to protect resources.

Another well-known example is a "SYN Flood" targeting TCP, whereby an attacker floods a server with SYN requests without any intent to complete the TCP handshake and establish a connection. This overloads TCP's connection table, potentially denying connections to legitimate clients. An Intrusion Detection System (see the next chapter) can help protect servers since a flood of SYN packets is anomalous behavior, but individual servers can also limit the impact by encoding connection state in the sequence number included in the SYN+ACK they send back to the client (a "SYN cookie" of sorts), and then allocate connection state only after the client goes to the trouble of correctly ACKing that packet. This is a variant of the first countermeasure in that it forces the attacker to use additional resources.

These examples are just a few of many illustrating the need to program defensively. This is especially true for protocols since they are designed to process messages from remote sources, exposing them to attempts to crash, hack, or as in the case of DoS attacks, simply consume the system. Defensive programming ventures outside the scope of this book, but the referenced OSDI paper illustrates one approach.

Further Reading:

X. Qie, R. Pang, and L. Peterson. Defensive Programming: Using an Annotation Toolkit to Build DoS-Resistant Software. Proceedings of the Fifth Symposium on Operating System Design and Implementation (OSDI). Usenix. December 2002.

Chapter 9. Firewalls

Whereas much of this book has focused on the uses of cryptography to provide such security features as authentication and confidentiality, there is a whole set of security issues that are not readily addressed by cryptographic means. For example, worms, viruses and other malware spread by exploiting bugs in operating systems and application programs (and sometimes human gullibility as well); no amount of cryptography can help you if your machine has unpatched vulnerabilities. So other approaches are often used to keep out various forms of potentially harmful traffic. Firewalls are one of the most common ways to do this.

To provide a little more context for this chapter, it is helpful to understand that writing software that is not vulnerable to being hacked is an important part of the overall security landscape. It is also a broad topic, starting with questions about the programming language you use (e.g., memory-safe languages like Rust are less susceptible than, say, C), and also including a variety of OS problems (e.g., how to efficiently enforce isolation between processes). Such topics are outside the scope of this book, where we instead take a network-centric view, and ask: *"What can we do in the network to either minimize opportunities for malware to exploit vulnerable software, or to mitigate the impact when such exploits succeed."* Firewalls, and more generally *security appliances*, are part of the answer. They are devices placed at strategic points throughout the network that identify and respond to malicious traffic.

The other big-picture takeaway is that firewalls and other security appliances illustrate the principle of defense in depth introduced in

Chapter 2. It would be ideal for all the software we run to be bulletproof, but for those times it isn't—e.g., when a new bug is discovered—we need a second line of defense. Network appliances play that role.

9.1 Basic Principles of Firewalls

The historical meaning of a firewall is a barrier to prevent the spread of fire from one part of a building to another. Firewalls are also present in many automotive vehicles to separate passengers from the noisy (and possibly fire-prone) engine compartment. Saltzer and Schroeder in 1975 applied the term, possibly for the first time in the context of computer security, when discussing least privilege.

A network firewall is a system that typically sits between two regions of a network, as illustrated in Figure 32, protecting the flow of traffic from one region to another. A common location would be a strategic point such as the ingress/egress point to an enterprise network or data center. Of course, unlike a physical firewall that blocks everything in its path, a network firewall is really a sort of packet filter that makes decisions about exactly what traffic is allowed to pass through it.

Historically, a firewall has been implemented as an "appliance": a dedicated system with one job, filtering packets. Firewalls have also been provided as a set of features available on a router, and a "personal firewall" may be implemented on an end-user machine. More recently (in the last decade or so), *distributed firewalls* have appeared in an effort to apply security policies to a greater amount of traffic. We return to this class of firewall later in the chapter.

Firewall-based security depends on the firewall being at some sort of choke-point. There should be no way to bypass the firewall via other gateways, or alternate paths such as wireless connections or dial-up connections. While the job of a firewall is to block potentially harmful traffic ("fire") for some definition of "harmful", a great deal of traffic passes through a firewall. One common setting for a firewall is "default closed": by default it blocks traffic unless that traffic is specifically allowed to pass through. For example, it might filter out all incoming messages except those addressed to a particular set of IP addresses and to particular TCP port numbers. Given the complexity of the environments where firewalls are used, with perhaps thousands of IP addresses and hundreds of applications in use, the configuration of firewalls also often becomes complex.

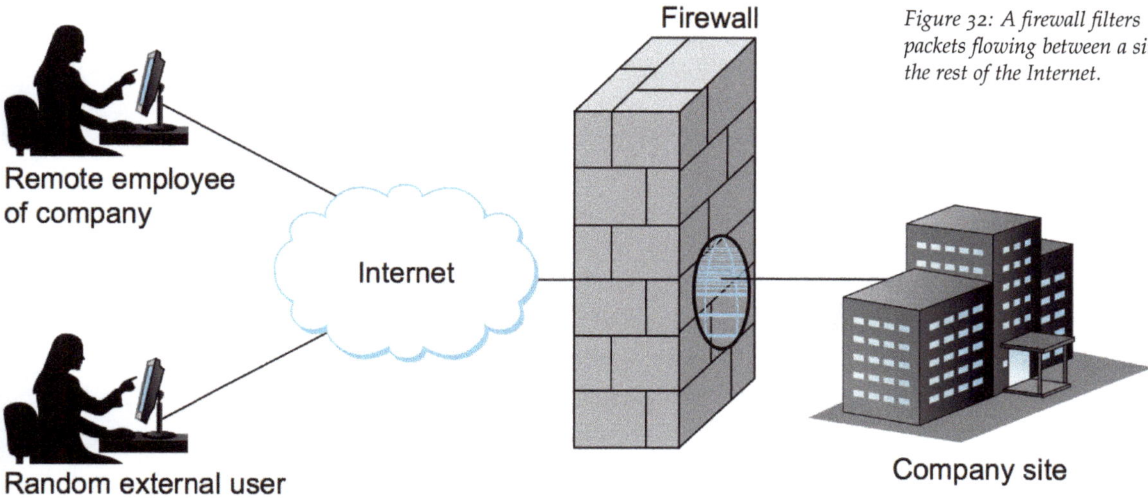

Figure 32: A firewall filters packets flowing between a site and the rest of the Internet.

When deployed at an ingress/egress point, a firewall divides a network into a more-trusted zone on one side of the firewall (the "inside") and a less-trusted zone that is "external" to the firewall. This is useful if, for example, you do not want external users to access a particular host or service within your site. Much of the complexity comes from the fact that you want to allow different kinds of access to different external users, ranging from the general public, to business partners, to remotely located members of your organization. A firewall may also impose restrictions on outgoing traffic to prevent certain attacks and to limit losses if an adversary succeeds in getting access inside the firewall (or to limit the damage of insider attacks).

The location of a firewall often happens to also be the dividing line between globally addressable regions and those that use local addresses. Hence, Network Address Translation (NAT) functionality and firewall functionality often are found in the same device, even though they are logically separate.

While the example above suggests a trusted and an untrusted network, firewalls are often used to create multiple *zones of trust*, such as a hierarchy of increasingly trusted zones. A common arrangement involves three zones of trust: the internal network, the *DMZ* ("demilitarized zone"); and the rest of the Internet. The DMZ is used to hold services such as DNS and email servers that need to be accessible to the outside. Both the internal network and the outside world can access the DMZ, but hosts in the DMZ cannot access the internal network; therefore, an adversary who succeeds in compromising a host in the exposed DMZ still cannot access the internal network. The DMZ can be periodically restored to a clean state.

Firewalls filter traffic based on information that can be found in the packets passing through them. This is likely to include such fields as IP addresses, the TCP or UDP port numbers, and so on. They are configured with a table of values in these fields that characterize the packets they will, and will not, forward. Generally, each entry in the table is a 4-tuple or 5-tuple: It gives the IP address and TCP (or UDP) port number for both the source and destination (four fields), and it may also include the specific value of the layer 4 protocol (TCP, UDP, etc.).

For example, a firewall might be configured to filter out (not forward) all packets that match the following description:

```
(198.51.100.14, 1234, 192.0.2.11, 80, TCP)
```

This pattern says to discard all TCP packets from port 1234 on host 198.51.100.14 addressed to port 80 on host 192.0.2.11. (Port 80 is the well-known TCP port for HTTP.) Of course, it's often not practical to name every source host whose packets you want to filter, so the patterns can include wildcards. For example,

```
(*,  *, 192.0.2.11, 80, TCP)
```

says to filter out all packets addressed to port 80 on 192.0.2.11, regardless of what source host or port sent the packet. Notice that address patterns like these require the firewall to make forwarding/filtering decisions based on level 4 port numbers, in addition to level 3 host addresses. For this reason, network layer firewalls are sometimes called *level 4 switches*.

Linux has a firewall feature called ufw (uncomplicated firewall) that can apply firewall rules on a host. We can implement the policy described above with the following command:

```
$ sudo ufw deny to 192.0.2.11 port 80
rule added
$
```

Then we can check that our rule was applied correctly:

```
$ sudo ufw status
Status: active

To                          Action       From
--                          ------       ----
192.0.2.11 80               DENY         Anywhere

$
```

In the preceding discussion, the firewall forwards everything except where specifically instructed to filter out certain kinds of packets. A firewall could also filter out everything unless explicitly instructed to forward it, or use a mix of the two strategies. For example, instead of blocking access to port 80 on host 192.0.2.11, the firewall might be instructed to block everything except access to port 25 (the SMTP mail port) on a particular mail server, such as

```
(*,  *, 198.51.100.9, 25)
```

We can specify this behavior with ufw:

```
$ sudo ufw default deny incoming
Default incoming policy changed to 'deny'
(be sure to update your rules accordingly)
$ sudo ufw allow to 198.51.100.9 port 25
rule added
```

```
$ sudo ufw status
Status: active

To                         Action      From
--                         ------      ----
198.51.100.9 25            ALLOW       Anywhere
```

Experience has shown that firewalls are very frequently configured incorrectly, allowing unsafe access, or breaking applications that need access. Part of the problem is that filtering rules can overlap in complex ways, making it hard for a system administrator to correctly express the intended filtering. A design principle that we discussed in Chapter 2 comes into play here: fail-safe defaults. The application of that principle to firewalls says they should, by default, discard all packets other than those that are explicitly allowed. Of course, this means that some valid applications might be accidentally disabled; the typical approach is that users of those applications eventually notice the breakage and ask the system administrator to make the appropriate change.

Many client/server applications dynamically assign a port to the client. If a client inside a firewall initiates access to an external server, the server's response would be addressed to the dynamically assigned port. This poses a problem: how can a firewall be configured to allow an arbitrary server's response packet but disallow a similar packet for which there was no client request? This is not possible with a *stateless firewall*, which evaluates each packet in isolation. It requires a *stateful firewall*, which keeps track of the state of each connection. An incoming packet addressed to a dynamically assigned port would then be allowed only if it is a valid response in the current state of a connection on that port.

Modern firewalls also understand and filter based on many specific application-level protocols such as HTTP or FTP. They use information specific to that protocol, such as URLs in the case of HTTP, to decide whether to discard a message. When firewalls are able to inspect payloads that are inside the TCP header (for example, to parse an HTTP request), this is referred to as *deep packet inspection* (DPI). Of course, DPI can be a challenge if end-to-end encryption is used.

A particular type of firewall that can interpret application traffic is the *Web Application Firewall*. Such firewalls are often placed directly in front of servers delivering web applications (or are implemented as a module within the server). They inspect the application traffic and apply filtering rules to identify and block specific attacks that target known vulnerabilities, such as SQL injection. When TLS is in use (as it invariably is in the modern web), web application firewalls terminate the HTTPS connection so that the application payload can be inspected. The open source ModSecurity project is a widely-used example of a web application firewall.

9.2 *Strengths and Weaknesses of Firewalls*

At best, a firewall protects a network from undesired access from the rest of the Internet; it cannot provide security to legitimate communication between the inside and the outside of the firewall. In contrast, the cryptography-based security mechanisms described in this chapter are capable of providing secure communication between any participants anywhere. This being the case, why are firewalls so common? One reason is that firewalls can be deployed unilaterally (by a network administrator, for example), using individual commercial products, while cryptography-based security requires support at both endpoints of the communication. A more fundamental reason for the dominance of firewalls is that they encapsulate security in a centralized place, in effect factoring security out of the rest of the network. A system administrator can manage the firewall to provide security, freeing the users and applications inside the firewall from security concerns—at least some kinds of security concerns. And as noted at the start of the chapter, encryption and authentication offer limited protection against exploitation of bugs in the operating systems of hosts.

Unfortunately, firewalls have serious limitations. Since a firewall does not restrict communication between hosts that are on the same side of the firewall, the adversary who does manage to gain access to one host at a site potentially has access to all local hosts. How might an adversary gain access inside the firewall? The adversary could be a disgruntled employee with legitimate access, or the adversary's software could be hidden in some software installed from a USB drive or downloaded from the Web. It might be possible to bypass the firewall by using a VPN—this has proven to be a common form of attack in recent years.

A related problem is that any parties granted access through your firewall, such as business partners or externally located employees, become a security vulnerability. If their security is not as good as yours, then an adversary could penetrate your security by penetrating their security.

While part of the motivation for firewalls is to protect machines that may have vulnerabilities from attack, their ability to do so is limited. If, for example, an attacker is able to gain access to a machine inside the firewall via one of the methods mentioned above, they may then be able to connect to another machine inside the firewall that contains an unpatched vulnerability, even though that machine itself is not directly accessible through the firewall. System administrators are expected to monitor for new vulnerabilities and patch them, but there is always a chance the vulnerabilities appear faster than then can be remediated. While staying up to date with patches is a best practice, it is certainly not one that is followed uniformly.

In Chapter 1 we discussed the threat posed by viruses, worms, and the general category of malware. While firewalls aim to stop the spread of malware, it can be a difficult task, since many operations that the firewall needs to permit, such as web browsing or email delivery, can also be used for the delivery of malware.

One approach that is used to detect malware is to search for segments of code from known malware, sometimes called a *signature*. This approach has its own challenges, as cleverly designed malware can tweak its representation in various ways. There is also a potential impact on network performance to perform such detailed inspection of data entering a network.

Some of the limitations of firewalls are related to the assumption that all traffic has to be funneled through a single appliance (or a small number of them). This leads to challenges both in performance, since so much traffic passes through a single choke point, and in effectiveness, since there can be plenty of traffic within an enterprise or a data center that has no need to pass through such a choke point. These limitations have led to the development of *distributed firewalls*, which we discuss in the following section.

9.3 Distributed Firewalls

A conventional firewall is implemented as a *choke point:* the network is set up in such a way that traffic must pass through the firewall to get from one part of the network to another. It is common to talk about devices as being "inside" or "outside" the firewall based on which side of that choke point they sit on. There are two implications of such an approach. One is that any devices that sit on the same side of the firewall are free to communicate with each other uninterrupted by the firewall. The second is that there must be an impenetrable barrier around the devices that are "inside" the firewall, with the firewall being the only way to get through that barrier. This seems appealing if you are trying to secure, say, the machines inside a single building, with only one connection to the outside world, but it becomes a lot less attractive if we are talking about securing all the machines in a complex enterprise spread across many sites. Even in simple cases, people find ways around a firewall. Once upon a time you might have to worry about an unsanctioned dial-up connection bypassing a firewall, while wireless networks and users at the ends of VPN tunnels are a bigger issue in contemporary settings. In any case, the concept of an impenetrable perimeter can be very difficult to sustain in practice.

The fact that a perimeter firewall does not filter traffic between machines on the same side of the firewall has enabled a set of attacks that make use of *lateral movement*. The core idea is that an attacker obtains a foothold in one system *inside* the firewall and then uses that as a base of operations to move around to the ultimate target. The initial system that the attacker breaches may not be particularly important. Perhaps he gains access via a phishing attack or by leveraging a vulnerability in the OS. But at this point the firewall is of no use, and the attacker can start trying to find ways to move from one system to another inside the firewall, until eventually he has access to a machine of interest, such as one holding sensitive data. These types of lateral movement attacks are extremely common and have been well documented, often lasting for months before they are detected.

The obvious solution to problems of lateral movement would seem to be internal firewalls. However, such a solution raises a new set of challenges. Consider the example in Figure 33, in which a single firewall has been deployed to filter traffic flows among a set of virtual machines in a datacenter.

Suppose that traffic sent from VM A to VM C needs to be processed at the firewall. To ensure it is filtered, traffic needs to be routed over a path that traverses the firewall, not necessarily the shortest path from A to C. In the more extreme case of traffic from VM A to VM B, the two VMs sit on the same host, so the traffic from A to B needs to be sent out of the host, across the network to the firewall, and then back to B. This is clearly not efficient, and consumes resources both within the network and at the network interface for the hairpinned traffic. Furthermore, the firewall itself has the potential to become a bottleneck, as all traffic requiring filtering must pass through to that centralized device.

Finally, there is considerable management overhead in supporting such an internal firewall. Assume that we start with some sensible default policies that deny all traffic flows aside from those explicitly allowed. Each new application that is deployed will require some new firewall rule to be created to allow traffic to flow between the component machines for that application. If a VM is moved, we may need to update the routing and the firewall rules to ensure that traffic continues to be filtered correctly. All of these concerns have led to internal firewalls being used rather sparingly.

The solution to the many issues with internal firewalls appeared as one of the features of network virtualization, the distributed firewall. Figure 34 illustrates a distributed firewall implementation. In this case, traffic sent from VM A to VM C can be processed by a firewall function at either (or both) of the virtual switches that it traverses, and still be sent over the shortest path through the network underlay between the two hosts, without hairpinning to a centralized firewall. Furthermore, traffic from VM A to VM B need never even leave the

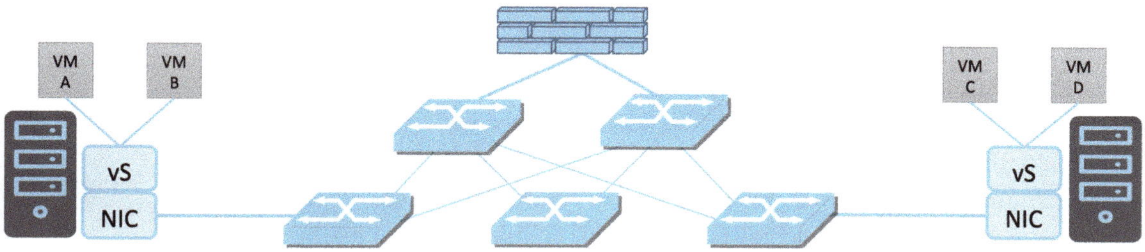

Figure 33: A single firewall in a virtualized datacenter.

host on which those two VMs reside, passing only through the virtual switch on that host to receive the necessary firewall treatment.

A significant side effect of distributing a service in this way is that there is no longer a central bottleneck. Every time another server is added to host some more VMs, there is a new virtual switch with capacity to do some amount of distributed processing. This means it is relatively simple to scale out the amount of firewalling in this way.

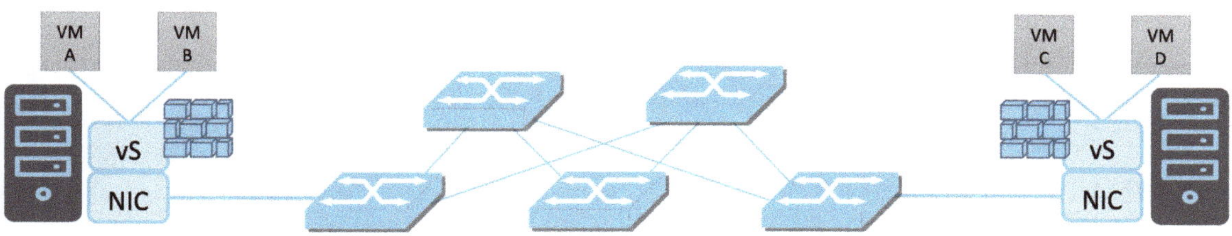

Figure 34: A distributed firewall is implemented as part of the virtual switch in every host in a datacenter.

A detail that we have glossed over up to this point is that the distributed firewall needs to be configured somehow. It would be intractable to configure firewall policies in every single virtual switch throughout a data center. This is why distributed firewalls appeared as a feature of software-defined networks. The SDN controller provides a central point of administrative control for firewall policies, while the implementation of filtering rules is distributed out to the virtual switches. Thus, for example, a rule that specifies how traffic from VM A to VM B should be filtered can be expressed to the SDN controller, which then calculates how to create the low level filtering rules to push out to the appropriate virtual switches. The SDN controller can also take account of such events as the migration of a VM from one location to another, or the addition of a new VM that requires additional firewall rules to be installed.

The approach described above is often referred to as *micro-segmentation*. By contrast to traditional firewall approaches in which large network segments offer unfettered access among all devices on the segment, micro-segmentation creates small and precisely defined virtual networks that connect only those systems that need to be able to communicate to deliver a particular service or function.

For further details on network virtualization and distributed services we recommend our companion book on software-defined networks.

Further Reading:

L. Peterson, C. Cascone, B. O'Connor, T. Vachuska, and B. Davie. Software-Defined Networks: A Systems Approach.

9.4 Zero Trust Security

As we noted above, traditional firewalls suffer from a fundamental weakness: they attempt to divide the network into "trusted" and "untrusted" zones. If an attacker manages to find a way to get access within the trusted zone, perhaps by compromising a legitimate piece of software running on the trusted side of the firewall, they now have a large set of machines on which to launch further attacks without interference. This state of affairs runs counter to some of the security principles we outlined in Chapter 2, notably the principle of least privilege. A machine on the trusted side of a firewall often has access to a lot more resources—other machines and data—than is necessary to do its job. One of the main approaches to improve this state of affairs is known as "zero trust security".

The term "zero trust" has been in use for decades, but started to enter widespread use around 2009, helped by the analyst firm Forrester. The central idea behind zero trust is that, by default, every device and user should be untrusted. Each user and device then needs to authenticate itself to gain access to a precise set of services. There is no blanket "trust this device to access anything" policy. Zero trust stands in contrast to the old "perimeter security" model in which there is the idea of a trusted region within a perimeter protected by firewalls and an untrusted region outside the perimeter.

Zero trust is sufficiently well accepted that NIST has written a specification, which provides this helpful definition:

Zero trust... became the term used to describe various cybersecurity solutions that moved security away from implied trust based on network location and instead focused on evaluating trust on a per-transaction basis.

Further Reading:

S. Rose, O. Borchert, S. Mitchell, S. Connelly. Zero Trust Architecture. NIST, 2020.

The classic example of trust based on location would be sitting in an office connected to some corporate network. Such a network would, in the past, have allowed anyone connected to it to access to a wide set of servers and data, with the trust being assumed because the user had managed to get admitted to the building.

There is more to zero trust that just getting away from location-based access. As a motivating example, consider a traditional VPN server providing remote access to a corporate network. Once a remote user is authenticated to the server, they are given access to a broad set of "inside the perimeter" resources (machines, data, etc.) within the enterprise. In effect, the user and their device are now treated as "trusted" to access many different systems. Such an approach has been the cause of many published breaches of sensitive data. An infamous example involved a heating and cooling system contractor's VPN credentials being used to access a retailer's database of customer credit card data. By contrast, a zero trust approach would entail a precisely defined policy that authenticates the user and their device to only the systems that are needed for them to do their job.

Micro-segmentation, described above, was one of the early technologies created to help in the implementation of zero trust. Rather than allowing all machines in a large network segment to communicate freely, as was the case previously, micro-segmentation allows precisely defined policies to limit communication among a set of devices to just what is needed to deliver their intended function. For example, the systems related to heating and cooling don't need access to the systems where customer credit card details are stored. A default policy of no access can also be established, with explicit configuration then required to create precisely specified allowable communication patterns between specific devices.

The VPN example above provides motivation for a different approach to handling users and devices outside of the confines of a traditional office and outside the perimeter defenses. A well-known and comprehensive approach to rethinking the perimeter defense and

VPN model is Google's BeyondCorp, described in a 2014 paper in the further reading section below. It is both an approach used to implement zero trust at Google for employees accessing corporate resources and a service that enterprises can implement themselves.

The starting position for BeyondCorp is that the perimeter model no longer makes sense in a world of global connectivity, remote workers, and ubiquitous mobile devices. The name suggests moving "beyond corporate"—that is, moving away from the idea that there is a trusted corporate network inside a perimeter and than any user or device inside that perimeter should have access to everything on the corporate network. Instead, users and devices have to be authenticated and authorized to receive fine-grained access to specific resources, no matter what their location is.

A central aspect of BeyondCorp is that only "managed devices" get to access protected resources. These managed devices are all issued with their own certificates so that they can be authenticated. Before connecting to any service within the enterprise, the device connects to a proxy that can perform authentication. After a device has been authenticated, then the user also has to authenticate themselves using two-factor authentication, and the user's access privileges are looked up in a database. Thus, for example, engineers may have access rights to engineering systems such as code repositories, but not to finance or HR systems. Only after all these checks—device, user authentication, and user authorization—have passed does the connection get established between the client and the server. Device checks may include not only verifying the certificate on a device but also checking that its operating system is up to date or that it has relevant antivirus software installed.

There are several subtleties to BeyondCorp, but the core principal of zero trust it embodies is this: location inside a perimeter (or building) is not a reason to trust a device or user with access to a broad set of resources. Nor should a VPN tunnel grant access to all resources within the perimeter. Only after the user has been authenticated and their authorization checked can they access a specific resource. Although less memorable, another way to say "zero trust" might be "narrow and specific trust after authentication and authorization"

Further Reading:

C. Cunningham. A Look Back At Zero Trust: Never Trust, Always Verify. Forrester, 2020.

R. Ward and B. Beyer. BeyondCorp: A New Approach to Enterprise Security. ;login:, Usenix, 2014.

9.5. *Intrusion Detection and Prevention*

As introduced at the beginning of this chapter, *security appliances* are a generalization of firewalls. Such appliances are placed throughout the network, watching for and responding to unwanted traffic. The main challenge they face is how to distinguish between good and bad traffic. This section looks at two examples: an *intrusion detection systems* (IDS), and its sibling *intrusion prevention systems* (IPS).

These systems look for anomalous activity, such as an unusually large amount of traffic targeting a particular port number, which often signals a malicious attempt to probe for a vulnerability. When identified, the appliance either generates an alarm for network managers, or in some cases, is able to take immediate action to limit the damage.

A good example of an IPS is Snort, an open source project first published in 1999, having started life as an IDS, and now owned by Cisco. In its original incarnation, Snort provided a lightweight, rule-based packet filtering and capture tool based on Berkeley Packet Filters. The idea is that attacks, such as worms, have a recognizable signature—for example, a particular combination of header values or a unique byte-string embedded in the payload—and that the IDS can be programmed with a rule to recognize the attack traffic, and raise alerts when this happens. As an IPS, Snort now takes the additional step of blocking the attack.

Further Reading:

Snort: Open Source Intrusion Prevention System (IPS) (`https://snort.org/`).

Like firewalls, IDS and IPS need to see all the traffic traversing a network if they are to detect attacks, and so strategic placement is important. That leads to the same concerns about east-west traffic that we discussed above, and thus there are also distributed versions of these systems.

Identifying Unwanted Traffic

Our overview of security appliances could lead to the conclusion that decisions about whether traffic is legitimate or malicious is clear cut. It often is not, and there can be real consequences in both directions. For example, an overly aggressive IPS rule-set or anomaly detection heuristic could raise false positives, restricting legitimate traffic and

> *negatively impacting revenue. Too conservative, and malicious traffic could crowd out legitimate traffic.*
>
> *It is also the case that that "unwanted" is in the eye of the beholder. Network probes that are sometimes used in research, with the ultimate goal of improving the Internet in some way, are often flagged as malicious. Even a single unexpected UDP packet can trigger a cease-and-desist letter. In other situations, administrators want to ensure that a human (and not an automated crawler) is sending requests to their websites. There are "opt-out" conventions (e.g., adding a robots.txt file), but they depend on the good will of other actors. Some website administrators are now using Anubis, an open source web application firewall, to ensure that a human, and not an AI bot trying to scrape their content, is at other end of every HTTP request.*

For an IDS/IPS that uses packet signatures to be effective, the set of potential attacks need to have been spotted in the wild and analyzed so that suitable rules can be formulated. Sharing rules among a community of users helps to speed up this process, and commercial IDS/IPS systems typically come with a subscription to a frequently-updated rules database. (See the Snort website referenced above for an example set of community rules.)

Another approach to using signatures is to look for *anomalies*—patterns in the behavior of traffic that somehow stand out from "normal" and can be categorized as a potential attack. Clearly this approach is attractive in that novel attacks can be detected before they make it into a rule database. The hard part is achieving high detection accuracy. Anomaly detection typically relies on machine learning algorithms to classify traffic as "normal" or "anomalous". Because both signature-based and anomaly-based detection have their respective strengths and weaknesses, it is common to find both approaches used in modern IDS/IPS systems.

The proliferation of security appliances again highlights the principle of defense in depth. For example, if we had a perfect firewall, we might not require an IDS or IPS. However, knowing that firewalls will never block all forms of malicious traffic leads to the conclusion that an IDS/IPS is worth having as a second line of defense.

About The Book

Read the Book

This book is part of the Systems Approach Series, with an online version published at `https://security.systemsapproach.org`.

To track progress and receive notices about new versions, you can follow the project on Mastodon. To read a running commentary on how the Internet is evolving, and for updates on our writing projects, you can sign up for the Systems Approach newsletter.

Build the Book

To build a web-viewable version, you first need to download the source:

```
$ mkdir ~/systemsapproach
$ cd ~/systemsapproach
$ git clone https://github.com/SystemsApproach/security.git
$ cd security
```

The build process is stored in the Makefile and requires Python be installed. The Makefile will create a virtualenv (venv-docs) which installs the documentation generation toolset. You may also need to install the enchant C library using your system's package manager for the spelling checker to function properly.

To generate HTML in _build/html, run make html. To check the formatting of the book, run make lint. To check spelling, run make spelling. If there are additional words, names, or acronyms that are correctly spelled but not in the dictionary, please add them to the dict.txt file. To see the other available output formats, run make.

Contribute to the Book

We hope that if you use this material, you are also willing to contribute back to it. If you are new to open source, you might check out the *How to Contribute to Open Source* guide (`https://opensource.guide/how-to-contribute/`). Among other things, you'll learn about issuing *Pull Requests* to merge your improvements back into GitHub.

About The Authors

Larry Peterson and Bruce Davie have been collaborating on systems projects and writing networking textbooks since the 1990s. Their book *Computer Networks: A Systems Approach*, a staple of networking curricula for the last 30 years, is now in its sixth edition. That introductory textbook, along with several new books focused on emerging topics in network and cloud systems, are available as open source at `https://systemsapproach.org`.

Larry spent most of his career in academia, first at the University of Arizona and later at Princeton University, where he was the Robert E. Kahn Professor of Computer Science. While at Princeton he directed the PlanetLab Consortium, building a global testbed for research on Internet-scale services. A CDN startup he helped spin out of PlanetLab was acquired by Akamai in 2010. In 2013 Larry transitioned to Emeritus status at Princeton and joined the Open Networking Lab (now the Open Networking Foundation) where he served as CTO, leading the design of open source platforms for Software-Defined Networking (SDN) and edge cloud computing. He currently chairs the Technical Steering Team for Aether, a Private 5G Project of the Linux Foundation. He is a member of the National Academy of Engineering, a Fellow of the ACM and the IEEE, the 2010 recipient of the IEEE Kobayashi Computer and Communication Award, and the 2013 recipient of the ACM SIGCOMM Award. He currently lives in Tucson Arizona.

Bruce began his networking career at Bellcore where he worked on the Aurora Gigabit testbed, which led to his first collaboration with Larry on high-speed host-network interfaces. He then went to Cisco where he led a team of architects responsible for Multiprotocol Label Switching (MPLS). He worked extensively at the IETF on standardizing MPLS and various quality of service technologies. Bruce also spent five years as a visiting lecturer at the Massachusetts Institute of Technology. In 2012 he joined Software Defined Networking (SDN) startup Nicira as a lead architect and was then a principal engineer at VMware following the acquisition of Nicira. In 2017 he took on the role of VP and CTO for the Asia Pacific region at VMware, which gave him the opportunity to return to Australia. He is a Fellow of the ACM and chaired ACM SIGCOMM from 2009 to 2013. He received the ACM SIGCOMM award in 2025.

www.ingramcontent.com/pod-product-compliance
Lightning Source LLC
LaVergne TN
LVHW070854210926
848482LV00016B/931